STUDIES IN CHURCH MUSIC AND LITURGY

JOSEPH GELINEAU

LITURGICAL ASSEMBLY
LITURGICAL SONG

PASTORAL
PRESS
PORTLAND · OREGON

Liturgical Assembly, Liturgical Song is the English Translation

of

Libres Propos sur les Assemblées Liturgiques © 1999 Les Éditions de l'Atelier/Éditions Ouvrières, Paris.
Translation by Paul Inwood.

and of

Les Chants de la Messe dans Leur Enracinement Rituel © 2001 Les Éditions du Cerf, Paris.
Translation by Bernadette Gasslein.

ISBN 1-56929-044-X

© 2002 Pastoral Press

Pastoral Press
A division of OCP Publications
5536 NE Hassalo
Portland, OR 97213
Phone 1-800-LITURGY (548-8749)
E-mail: liturgy@ocp.org
Website: www.ocp.org
All rights reserved
Printed in the United States of America

Managing Editor: Glenn CJ Byer
Assistant Editor: Melissa C. Phong
Editorial Assistance: Michael Kasner

Publisher: John J. Limb
Editorial Director: Paulette McCoy
Book Design: Judy Urben
Cover Design: Le Vu
Art Direction: Jean Germano
Cover Art: Giotto di Bondone (1266-1336). Coronation of the Virgin (Baroncelli polyptych).
        Cappella Baroncelli, S. Croce, Florence, Italy
        Copyright Scala / Art Resource, NY

TABLE OF CONTENTS

Editor's Introduction

This book presents two works by Joseph Gelineau, S.J., in a single volume. The first deals with the state of the liturgical assembly some thirty years after the reforms of the Second Vatican Council brought into focus the importance of the gathered people of God. The second deals with the place of song within that assembly.

When Fr. Gelineau looks with the eye of a theologian, critical yet hopeful, at the way we gather, he brings before us the challenge to live out the call that comes from our baptism. The assembly is a gathering filled with meaning, most of which comes from the baptismal call of all the faithful. In his opinion anything that does not build up this body is a cause for concern. When he examines the role of music in the celebration, the musicologist shows the magnificent palette of music from which we need to draw in order to support what the assembly is called to do. In his challenge to those who seek monolithic assemblies and mono-phonic sound, the historian shows that the assembly and its song have been as varied as the people who have been sealed with the cross of Christ. Finally, he shows that music and assembly are not to be analyzed as separate realities, for as long as there has been church there has been song.

For all these reasons and more, these two works are presented as a single opus in English. In making this translation we have tried to preserve the voice of the author as much as the message. For this reason the reader will find paragraph structures and occasional turns of phrase that may seem out of the ordinary.

It is my hope that the insights of each work will be deepened by the reading of the other, and that the challenge found on each page will sound with ever greater insistence for the equation of the *liturgical assembly* with its *liturgical song*.

Glenn CJ Byer, MA SLD
May 23, 2002

Abbreviations

GIRM   *General Instruction of the Roman Missal*

IGRM 2000   *Institutio Generalis Missalis Romani, 2000*
LMD   *La Maison-Dieu*
MNA   *Missel noté de l'assemblée*
PL   *Patrologiae cursus completes, series Latina,* Migne

A, AL, B, D, F, I, L, Z all refer to the French system known as *fiches de chant* which uses categories and numbers to identify sheet music.

BOOK ONE

REFLECTIONS ON RENEWAL

PREFACE

In this book, Fr. Joseph Gelineau gives us his personal reflections on liturgical assemblies today, a subject he has been passionate about for a very long time and a subject which more than ever is at the heart of the church's preoccupations. A significant change of perspective flowed from the Second Vatican Council. Until then, the liturgy had been perceived and put into practice as a kind of "cultic worship to be rendered unto God," obligatory for Christians; but now it has rediscovered its true ecclesial dimension. To go to Mass is above all to go to join the assembly, to give a concrete face and substance to a local church which welcomes and celebrates the "grace of Jesus the Savior, the love of God the Father and the fellowship of the Holy Spirit" in order to live this out in daily life. Fr. Gelineau takes a fresh look at the meaning of the Christian assembly, what is at stake now that it has once again found its true place in the life of the church; and he opens up real vistas for the practices of today's Christians. What sort of forms can assemblies take when their frequency is diminishing, and when — in French dioceses — different strategies for regrouping and restructuring are being carried out? To what new expectations should assemblies now be responding?

For 50 years, Joseph Gelineau has been one of the pioneers of the liturgical movement in France, and indeed throughout the world. As a brave and persevering viticulturist, he has tended the liturgical vine so that it might bring forth the best fruits, the best wine.

We are also in his debt for much else; for numerous papers on pastoral liturgy and liturgical music, for the rehabilitation of the psalms and the inventing of a way for them to be cantillated in the French tongue,* and for numerous hymns and other musical works — for Joseph Gelineau does not claim to have any other craft than "that of a composer."

---

* Fr. Gelineau's psalm tones wedded with the Grail Psalter also became popular in the English-speaking world. — Editor.

We should be especially grateful to him, and I am delighted to be able to testify personally to this, for his interest in, and passion for, everything that concerns the liturgy. He has truly been a stimulus to missions in the fields of liturgical music and reflections on pastoral practice, and he has also contributed to drawing together all those who serve the liturgy. He organized and edited the symposium *Dans vos assemblées* (Desclée, pp. 680) with the help of forty or so other writers. This compilation, which was issued in a substantially revised single-volume third edition in 1998, will remain a standard and invaluable work of reference for many years to come.

Joseph Gelineau has come to the writing of these *Reflections on Renewal* at the end of a long detour in his life. For seventeen years he had pastoral charge of five country parishes while still continuing his teaching activities. The chapters that follow are full of his personal experiences as well as of his personal culture. All those who know him, together with a large audience of other readers, will be able to appreciate the freedom of thought to be found behind his words, words that he offers to us in all simplicity as his legacy.

Michel Scouarnec

Chapter I

THE CHRISTIAN ASSEMBLY

"To the church of God that is at Corinth"
1 Corinthians 1:2*

At the end of the 1960s, a sociological survey was commissioned by a group called *Les Chantiers du Cardinal* ("The Cardinal's Workshop"). It posed the following question orally: "What does the word 'church' mean to you?" *Saying* the word 'church' maintained a deliberate ambiguity, since the presence or absence of a capital letter could not be detected in an oral question.

For the vast majority of those surveyed, the immediate response was in terms of the building, which can be found in every French village. For a minority, the word evoked the social institution, which denotes the members of one of the large Christian denominational groupings; Catholic, Orthodox or Protestant.

But there is another usage for this word that we see in the earliest Christian writings. In his two letters to the Christians of Corinth, the Apostle Paul addresses "the church of God that is at Corinth" (1 Corinthians 1:2; 2 Corinthians 1:2). This form is unusual to us: Paul was not addressing a building, nor is the whole church to be found in Corinth!

This invites us to reflect on the original meaning of the word *church*, for the re-establishment of the value of this meaning of the word has marked the entire liturgical renewal in our century.

---

* Scripture citations are from *The New American Bible with the Revised New Testament and Revised Psalms* (Washington, D.C.: Confraternity of Christian Doctrine, 1991). — Editor

THE REDISCOVERED ASSEMBLY

I will never forget my astonishment and amazement when I heard Canon A. G. Martimort talking about *the liturgical assembly* and *the* mysterion *of the assembly* during one of the first workshops organized by what was then, in 1948, the brand new *Centre de Pastorale Liturgique* (Center for Pastoral Liturgy) in Paris. Up to that time, for me the word *assembly* had only meant the annual village festival held on 24 June, a meaning immortalized in that marvelous song from my childhood:

It's the feast of St. John

that wonderful night

when lovers

go to the assembly [gathering].

Let's walk there too

with joy-filled hearts.

For the moon has risen![1]

Later I was to learn that the ceremonial books of the Latin rite written since the Middle Ages were only addressed to the ministers of worship and were not directly concerned with the assembly's participation. For that, we would have to wait ten centuries for Pope Pius XII's decree restoring the Easter Vigil to find this written about the readings at the Vigil: "The people listen." So the liturgy does presuppose an assembly!

THE FIRST VISIBLE SIGNS OF THE CHURCH

When you start to look closely at the writings of the New Testament and the early days of Christianity, you are struck by the importance given to the gathering of Christians. It began on the day of Pentecost when the disciples "were all in one place together" and, at the noise of a sudden rush of wind, a whole crowd "gathered" (Acts of the Apostles 2:1-6).

---

[1] *Voici la Saint Jean,*
la grande nuitée
où les amoureux
vont à l'assemblée:

Marchons, joli coeur,
la lune est levée!

For pagan commentators like Pliny the Younger, gathering on a fixed day was the primary characteristic marking out Christians. It was there that their persecutors found them; it was this that they were accused of, and this for which the martyrs of Abitina (put to death at Carthage in 304) proudly defended themselves when they faced the Roman governor:

> As if a Christian could exist without the Sunday assembly, and as if this day could be celebrated without Christians! One cannot exist without the other.[2]

The expression "the church…that is at" assumes its proper dimensions when we recall those myriad little Christian communities scattered all along the rim of the Mediterranean Sea. They existed in the midst of a pagan society. They were seen either as insignificant minorities that were ignored or deviant groups that were a nuisance and therefore persecuted. It was in their assemblies that these Christians found their true identity: they heard the liberating word, prayed and gave thanks, initiated new believers. They shared the bread of their Communion, and gave each other whatever help was needed. The life of the church then depended on its assemblies.

ERASURE OF THE SIGN OF THE ASSEMBLY

The relationship between assemblies of Christians and the surrounding society experienced two reversals in the course of history. In the 4th and 5th centuries, the church passed from being a persecuted minority to being the majority religion allied to the civil authorities. The second transition took place in the 19th and 20th centuries when Western culture devolved from a Christian society into a church scattered within a secularized world.

The first reversal took place when the church, until then persecuted by the Roman authorities, discovered an ally in the person of the emperor Constantine, who became a convert to Christianity. Little by little, Christianity became the state religion. As a result, Christians achieved a majority position around the rim of the Mediterranean as heathen chieftains had themselves baptized along with their entire tribes. Henceforth it was no longer a social anomaly to be baptized; rather it was the exception *not* to be baptized, as was the case with the Jews and the Moors.

---

[2] The martyr in question was Emeritus, who said, succinctly: *Sine dominica non possumus.* — Translator

The Christian religion organized itself territorially into dioceses and parishes. No longer would people refer to "the church…that is *at* X" but to "the church *of* X." Whether one participated or not in the Sunday assembly was no longer a major sign of belonging to the Christian religion; there were those who practiced and those who did not. But everyone, practicing or not, was part of the same civil and religious society.

After the Reformation, a European might be a Catholic or a Protestant depending on whether the local prince himself belonged to one denomination or another. Without a doubt, church society cohesiveness would suffer further shocks, such as secularization and religious indifference of the Age of Enlightenment. Still, until Vatican II the idea of Christendom formed the basis of the image of how the Catholic Church presented itself.

A NEW CHURCH-SOCIETY RELATIONSHIP

However, a large gulf opened up between the majority religion of the French nation and the social life of these same French people. In our society, marked by the movements of our time, secularization would henceforth be imposed on everyone.

Furthermore, from now on we have to distinguish between adherence to a religion and actual profession of Christian faith. Ever since we entered the free market era for religions, for beliefs, for churches and for sects, a specific relationship to the gospel has been eradicated and has disappeared, even if it remains in a diluted form in the socio-cultural behavior patterns of those who were once baptized as Christians.

Even if the *façade* of the Catholic Church in France is still impressive, with all its churches in towns and villages, its pilgrimages, its crosses and wayside Calvarys, its Christian place names, and so on — as well as through its schools, monasteries, convents and religious communities, charitable organizations, Catholic Action movements, and innumerable pious and devotional groups — the visible coherence of this entire heritage is falling apart at the seams. Churches are closed, rectories are sold, convents are disappearing, and good works are running out of steam. In addition to this visible recession we also see a correspondingly progressive decrease in the number of infants being baptized and a severe drop in the number of active clergy.

It was in this context that the Second Vatican Council restored a vision of the church where the sign of the local church would find a new reality.

THE SACRAMENT OF THE CHURCH

The contemporary liturgical movement, particularly in France during the 1940s and 1950s and onwards, had already rediscovered that the liturgy is the action of a people gathered together. It is for this assembly that the book is read and the bread is broken. It is this assembly that gives praise and offers supplication. The ground was therefore already prepared for the new view of the church that Vatican II would bring to the fore. In the *Dogmatic Constitution on the Church*, the church itself is described as a sacrament, in other words, a visible sign leading to an invisible reality.[3]

In the Greek word *ekklesia*,[4] as in the Hebrew *qahal* applied to the people of the covenant, there is an image of convocation, of being called together: Those who hear God's call gather themselves together. In the history of Judeo-Christian revelation, believers had specific assemblies related to their faith, the gatherings of "the people of Yahweh" at which the Covenant was renewed and, from Pentecost onwards, gatherings of those who had heard the Good News, who had responded to the call, and who kept watch until the master should return.

Thus, ever since there have been Christians, it is here that they are visible and identifiable. In particular gatherings, when they assemble together in a place and time that are always transitory, and in a location where they can recognize themselves as belonging to the invisible people of the redeemed. Wherever they are and however many they may be, the visible churches, together with the invisible kingdom that is to come, inseparably form the *mysterion* (sacrament) of the church.

SCATTERED CHURCHES

This vision of the assemblies of the church takes on a fresh importance at a time when these assemblies are gradually losing the privileges that controlled — and which still partly control — the Catholic ecclesial institution in French society.

Territorial partitioning is once again in question. Ancient parishes, often dating back to the time of Charlemagne, are being grouped together. Little by little we are regressing from "the church *of* X" back to "the church . . . that is gathered *at* X" — in other words, to the assembly of Christians which takes place on such-and-such a day in such-and-such a place. Although the sociological context is quite different, our current situation is not without its similarities to that of the scattered and persecuted church of the first centuries of Christianity.

---

[3] *Lumen Gentium* 1 and 9.
[4] From which the French word *église* (church) is derived.

The people found in our gatherings have a new face. In a traditional parish, there were primarily practicing Catholics, faithful to the Sunday Mass obligation, assured as they were of the stability of the rites, and handing over all responsibility for the celebration of these rites to those who were in charge of them: priests, cantors, servers, sacristans, etc. In the local regroupings of a scattered church, we primarily encounter Christians aware of their baptismal priesthood and motivated to take an active part in a communal celebration. They have come because they want to be there today. Some are involved in the local Christian community and look after the services without which it could not exist; others are occasional worshippers, others are catechumens, others have come to have a look; still others are just passing through. The local assembly is more diverse, more open, and more unpredictable.

CELEBRATION AND EVANGELIZATION

In this way, a strange opposition is being resolved — a dichotomy between a *missionary* church and a *worshiping* church, which marked the period from the 1930s to the 1960s. In order to evangelize, it was thought necessary first of all to emerge from our churches and rejoin the human race in the midst of its daily life, because the liturgy at that time was carried out by clerics on behalf of the baptized and catechized believers. To clerics was assigned the role of preparing worship for practicing believers. To militant lay people was assigned the role of impregnating the tasks of this world with the gospel.

Although the distinction between the two forces, one near the center and the other toward the periphery, is not without basis or meaning, today we can more easily see the danger of falling into a dichotomy. What sort of testimony would a baptized person who was cut off completely from the community of the church and its sacraments give to the world? On the other hand, we have noticed for a while now that the liturgy and its symbols, the gathering of believers who pray and celebrate together, has once again become for many whether baptized or not the primary and special *locus* where they are opened up to transcendence and to listening to the gospel word.

We are witnessing the birth of local assemblies that offer an image of believers at prayer that is more mobile, flexible, creative, affectionate, and welcoming. Their existence and their way of actually being give witness to an enlightened faith, to a way of praying that is both simple and true, to a sense of community and to a radiant joy. Their poverty, due to the small number of participants and their meager social standing, can even become an eloquent sign of the power of the Spirit that animates them.

Our assemblies are not without their faults and weaknesses, their grumblings and disagreements, any more than was the case with the Corinthian assembly to which Paul wrote in a tone of severe reproach; "for the Lord did not come for the just but for sinners, and to give confidence to his "little flock" (Luke 12:32).

The more the church is scattered,
the more its assemblies have meaning and value.

Chapter 2

SERVANTS IN THE ASSEMBLY

*"According to the gift
that each of you has received...."*

1 Peter 4:10

Among the first Christian communities, thanks to the two letters that the Apostle Paul wrote to them, we know the one at Corinth better than the others. Chapters 12 to 14 of the first letter show us how this church lived, thanks to the gifts that the Spirit distributed to the members of this social body, for the good of all and the good of each person.

The organization that the church adopted from the second century onward, especially with the functions of bishop, priests, and deacons, had not yet become the norm. But all that is necessary for the life of a local community is already present in a rich outburst from the great variety of gifts, given to each person, not for their own good but for the good of the group.

DIVERSITY OF GIFTS

Thus from the very beginnings of the church, we see activities taking place at the service of the Word, thanks to the apostles, the evangelists, prophets and prophetesses, teachers and so on. We see works of mercy, help and healing. We see works that build up the body, seers, gift of tongues, discernment, works of direction and of pastoral care which soon led to the institution of elders in all the churches. We also see how, after Paul had left Corinth, Stephanas and his family "devoted themselves to the service of the holy ones" (1 Corinthians 16:15).

Certain works of service would become more clearly defined as time passed. Some were for welcoming and accompanying catechumens on their journey (for example, the ministry of exorcism); others for the liturgy (lectors, psalmists, doorkeepers, subdeacons); still others for taking Communion to the sick and those absent and for spiritual counseling.

THE CLERGY IN POWER

With the dissolution of the Roman Empire and the mass conversion of barbarians into the church, the church actively collaborated in establishing a new social order. Between the civil power of kings and lords on the one hand, and an enslaved people on the other, the clergy and monks held the reins of overall spiritual power as well as cultural power and a significant amount of temporal goods. Without ceasing, the Spirit continued to awaken in the saints the multiple and diverse charisms needed for the good of the whole of society. But the overall life of the church depended on the clergy. All offices and powers were concentrated in their hands.

Despite the turbulences of history (the Reformation, the French Revolution, the emergence of a scientific and industrial civilization), the functioning of the institutions of the Catholic Church, institutions that are spread across dioceses and parishes, although increasingly centralized in Rome, has remained substantially the same.

THE CHURCH AS A COMMUNION

The Second Vatican Council was the herald and the promoter of a renewed mode of ecclesial life, whose key word is *communion*. In its most common usage, the word designates the act by which one participates in the Lord's Supper by eating the consecrated bread and thus becoming the Body of the Lord. The word is also commonly used when speaking about the feast of First Holy Communion.[5] But the expression "the communion of saints" encountered in the recitation of the creed remains a rather nebulous concept for many people.

Like the word *church*, the word *communion* has different uses that underline both the communal life of believers, shown to be a significant characteristic of the earliest Christians in the Acts of the Apostles (2:44-45), and the mystical union of those who are already members of the one Body of Christ. The word implies

---

[5] And, additionally in France, *communion solennelle*, a solemn receiving of Communion which normally takes place at the age of 12 or 13 and is both a rite of passage at about the time of puberty and a kind of commitment to the life of the church. It thus fulfills much of the role currently allotted to the sacrament of confirmation in other countries, where this is used as a sacrament of commitment on the way to adulthood. Like confirmation, this Solemn Communion is increasingly becoming, in effect, an occasion for young people to bid farewell to the church. — Translator

the nature proper to the church and to all the local churches. In *communion* we often hear the *union* part of the word when we really ought to be hearing the *common* or *communal* part of it.[6] Communion is what we have and what is lived in common, a global and existential solidarity.

> It is the Holy Spirit, dwelling in those who believe and pervading and ruling over the entire Church, who brings about that wonderful communion of the faithful and joins them together so intimately in Christ that he is the principle of the Church's unity. By distributing various kinds of spiritual gifts and ministries (cf. 1 Corinthians 12:4-11) he enriches the Church of Jesus Christ with different functions, "in order to perfect the saints for the work of service, so as to build up the body of Christ" (Ephesians 4:12).[7]

THE ASSEMBLY AS SIGN OF COMMUNION

Sometimes people depict the time we are living through now, in the wake of Vatican II, as a time of passing from a centralized and clerical church to a communion of local churches. One of the most visible places where this transformation can be observed is undoubtedly in the life of liturgical assemblies. Once Vatican II drew our attention to the "conscious, and active participation" of all the faithful gathered together, an irreversible movement was set in motion. We have now distanced ourselves from the age-old forms of worship consisting essentially of *ceremonies* under the sole charge of clerics, or their like, and celebrated before a *spectating* people. Now we are rediscovering the liturgy as the action of all the people assembled, who listen to the word, sing and pray together, receive Communion and share — even if certain roles are still the preserve of ordained, instituted or commissioned members, who are seen as servants of communion.

THE PROCLAIMED WORD

The most important and the most decisive effect of Vatican II was undoubtedly the fact of having "opened the book in the presence of the people" and thus allowing everyone to hear "in their own tongue" the word of God. The Bible is no longer reserved for clerics who know Latin. Now each person can drink at this wellspring and be nourished with this bread of life when it is shared in the faith of the church that is charged with breaking this bread of the word according to the capacity of each person to receive it. And this nourishing food does not reach us

---

[6] The wordplay of this comment works better in French: *Communion* — not so much of the *union*, rather more of the *commune* — is what is needed. — Translator

[7] *Unitatis redintegratio* (Decree on Ecumenism) 2. Except where noted, conciliar citations are from A. Flannery, ed., *Vatican II: The Conciliar and Post Conciliar Documents* (Liturgical Press: Collegeville, MN, 1975). — Editor

only through those with doctorates in biblical science, but can also reach us via an individual simple soul under the enlightening influence of the Holy Spirit.

THE PRIESTHOOD OF THE BAPTIZED

Another notable fruit of Vatican II was the progressive rediscovery by lay people of the common priesthood of their baptism, which makes them "priests, prophets, and kings" in Christ. Thus it is that we see in every area of the life of the church that lay people are involving themselves in ever-increasing numbers. Of course, in every age there arose in the church men and women who, under the action of the Spirit, undertook a permanent life of prayer, formed children in the faith, came together to support each other in living the gospel and looked after the sick and the marginalized in society. But none of this impinged on the exercise of power reserved to clerics. The novelty for us is that those who are merely baptized and not ordained are taking part, as baptized people, in areas that were formerly off-limits to them, such as catechesis, preaching, liturgy and organization of the local church.

NEW MINISTRIES

This evolution has not been without its tensions, however. It is always a perilous thing to touch on anything that has to do with institutions of power. In 1972, understanding as he did the growing need for real ministries entrusted to the baptized in the life of the church after Vatican II, Pope Paul VI opened up new pathways. Taking his inspiration from the two ancient minor orders of lector and acolyte, he created two instituted ministries: the *Service of the Word* and the *Service of the Eucharist*. Paradoxically, in a country like France* where there is a high proportion of lay people who are involved and have responsibility in the church, this prophetic initiative has had practically no effect, either on lay people or on their bishops. Why not?

The fact that these ministries were open only for people of the male sex was certainly a shock in an era when women were already fulfilling many roles of service in the liturgy. But there was an even greater malaise. What caused this? Was there a lack of precision in what was proposed? A fear on the part of lay people of becoming clericalized? A fear on the part of priests of seeing their identity shaken through losing some of the activities which seemed to them to be part of their *raison d'être*? A fear that new ministries would dry up priestly vocations that were already only a trickling stream? Was it rather a supercilious theology, very much anchored in the unbreachable boundary of the sacrament of orders and of

---

* This has also been true throughout the English-speaking world. — Editor

the ministerial priesthood? Was it a hardening of Rome's attitude in the 1980s on the whole question of the ministry of lay people? Was it a lack of audacity to innovate by lay people in positions of responsibility, or the lack of a clear vision to follow? Was it the lack of determination by clergy and bishops to support these ministries? Without a doubt it was a combination of all these factors and the overall effect was paralysis.

Wisdom will not come from decisions made on high but in the needs that are most obvious and from everything that is already being done in order to best respond to them. The issue here is no longer a quibble over whether or not a baptized person can deliver a homily in an assembly. Rather, it is a question of welcoming the word of these numerous lay people who have undergone formation, those who know how to give a teaching based on scripture, a teaching that is both solid and appropriate to the level of the listeners, or who know how to provide a deep meditation, taking as its starting point the demands of the gospel in our concrete daily lives. It's a question of entrusting those who walk alongside catechumens with the different rites of the RCIA, including the scrutinies. It's a question of no longer feeling panicked when those dangerously ill or dying ask the layman or laywoman who is visiting them to grant pardon for all their sins, since the man or woman can always say something like, "God always forgives those who sincerely ask for pardon. Let us ask him for this grace together, in trust and confidence."

Nor is it any longer the hour to erect barriers around catechists, leaders of prayer groups and leaders of Sunday assemblies by constantly telling them, "Never forget that you aren't priests!" Rather, it's a question of reflecting with them on the best way of helping their brothers and sisters, believers or those who want to believe, each serving them according to the gift that they have received and the works of service for which they have been prepared.

If all this can happen in the mutual confidence of bishops, priests and baptized people, things will move forward rapidly. Deacons, who are often caught in the middle, will also be better able to find their ecclesial and personal identity. Lay people will be able to see themselves as fully integrated members of the local church.

The better that gifts and works of service
are shared in the assembly,
the better the action of the Holy Spirit will be manifested.

CHAPTER 3

WHAT MAKES UP THE ASSEMBLY

*"Devoted to teaching,
to the prayers, to the sharing"*

Acts of the Apostles 2:42

At the beginning of the book of the Acts of the Apostles, Luke describes the way in which the first Christian community in Jerusalem lived. It was not only a question of describing something in the past; it was at the same time a program for the churches to follow in the centuries to come.

Just to remind us of this frequently cited passage:

The disciples devoted themselves to the teaching of the Apostles, to the fellowship, to the sharing of bread, and to the prayers...and they held all their possessions in common (Acts of the Apostles 2:42-44).

The first characteristic we see is the word as a proclamation of the Good News as an exhortation to conversion, as teaching and as encouragement. Next in order we meet *koinônia* (communion), which undoubtedly denotes a life of fellowship but also participation in the life of Christ in the whole of his mystical body through the workings of the Holy Spirit. Third comes the sharing of the bread, which is *par excellence* the eucharistic meal in memory of the Lord. Last are the prayers by which all religious confession of faith exists and is signified. The strong emphasis on the sharing of possessions is linked to the three preceding signs.

HISTORICAL VARIATIONS

This ideal program for life in the church was realized and lived out in very different ways over the centuries, depending on time and place. Variations were sometimes considerable in the case of the word when evangelization was done from the starting point of the life of the saints rather than from the Bible or the Eucharist when, for centuries, only the priest received Communion at the majority of Masses. Throughout the history of the church, the two points that remained the most obvious were mutual charitable help and the prayers. What is the position today, more than thirty years after Vatican II?

IN A LOCAL COMMUNITY

A passage from John Paul II's encyclical *Redemptoris Missio* can help us in our reflection:

> A rapidly growing phenomenon in the young churches - one sometimes fostered by the bishops and their Conferences as a pastoral priority - is that of 'ecclesial basic communities' (also known by other names) which are proving to be good centers for Christian formation and missionary outreach. These are groups of Christians who, at the level of the family or in a similarly restricted setting, come together for prayer, Scripture reading, catechesis, and discussion on human and ecclesial problems with a view to a common commitment. These communities are a sign of vitality within the Church, an instrument of formation and evangelization, and a solid starting point for a new society based on a 'civilization of love....'

Thus, these communities become a means of evangelization and of the initial proclamation of the Gospel, and a source of new ministries. At the same time, by being imbued with Christ's love, they also show how divisions, tribalism and racism can be overcome.[8]

ASSEMBLIES IN THE ABSENCE OF A PRIEST

These words of John Paul II refer first of all to regions such as Latin America or English-speaking Africa, where base communities have flourished. However, this phenomenon is not unrelated to the "Sunday Assemblies in the Absence of a Priest" which appeared in France and elsewhere in the course of the 1970s.

---

[8] *Redemptoris Missio* 51.

The church of X or Y finds itself deprived of its Sunday Mass. This church knows that if it renounces the Sunday assembly, it is actually local Christian life that is imperiled; it would be a church scattered. In fact, the irregular regrouping for Eucharist of communities in a particular area supports only a minority of committed Christians. This solution tends to sideline children, old people, occasional churchgoers, inquirers and so on. Because of these pitfalls, a new type of local church life comes into being.

These Sunday Assemblies in the Absence of a Priest (SAAPs)[9] have caused problems and have often been perceived as an anomaly given the ancient axiom, no church without Eucharist. And, in order that we may not forget it, the official title for these Sunday assemblies necessarily includes the qualification "*without a priest.*"* In some dioceses, lay people have been supported and trained for involvement in this area. In others, people have been more or less left to fend for themselves. In some cases, bishops have forbidden such assemblies or suppressed them after they had been used.

It is still too early to analyze twenty-five years of SAAPs. As a priest actively engaged in this movement, I can testify that I have seen the power of the Holy Spirit working in it. Baptized people have found a new dimension to their baptism, new ministers have sprung up, and little ecclesial communities have been born similar to the churches in communion that Vatican II desired.** But another current has also been evident in the evolution of assemblies of Christians in the Catholic Church in France.

REGROUPING OF PARISHES

The evolving movement toward SAAPs is a decentralized movement stemming from the grassroots. A quite different movement in the opposite direction, coming down from bishops and diocesan administrators, favors clusters of parishes. In the wake of population shifts, which have emptied some rural areas and contributed to the growth of new towns, and in the wake of a serious diminution in the number of priests in active ministry, paralleled by the decline in Mass attendance by practicing Catholics, something had to be done. With some notable exceptions, a significant number of dioceses has carried out

---

[9] In French, ADAP (*Assemblée Dominicale en l'Absence de Prêtre*). In England, the acronym SWAP is sometimes found — Sunday Worship in the Absence of a Priest — but this term is based on what the people do (worship) rather than on who they are (people gathered together). — Translator

* In the United States the ritual book for these assemblies is called *Sunday Celebrations in the Absence of a Priest* and in Canada, *Sunday Celebrations of the Word and Hours.* — Editor

** It is to be noted that the author is dealing here with *Sunday* assemblies. In many English-speaking parts of the world, "eucharistic services" or "services of the word and Communion" are becoming common on weekdays also. The wisdom of this development is the subject of ongoing debate. — Translator

regroupings of parishes around new centers where the clergy and other resources for the area are situated.

By suppressing parishes, and in part alienating the church buildings, how have we taken into account the necessity for the church's presence in the places where families and individuals live, many of whom find it difficult to come together in a more distant center? This concern does not always appear as a clear priority for our mission. Sometimes one gets the impression of an administrative recentralization and a strategy of retrenchment in order to ensure bare survival.

CENTER AND PERIPHERY

We seem to be in the presence of two different conceptions of how to build the church of tomorrow. One implicitly maintains the vision inherited from a millennium of Christianity. Everything depends on the bishops, the priests, the Sunday Mass, and the sacred moments of life, from birth to death. The other conception favors the witness of an ecclesial base community. Although small, they are seen as the priority for mission and evangelization, even if it is not yet possible to put in place all the functions that one would desire for a base community. In fact the local church, in the full meaning of the word, remains the diocese, which by its nature is the total church in one of its parts.

Without a doubt it is easier to discern from the viewpoint of a base community that the major missing link for the growth of the church is Christian initiation. This is what needs to be restored and revitalized as a matter of first priority. It is through Christian initiation that we come to the Eucharist and to the necessity for ordained ministers in a diocesan church, gathered around a local bishop.

ASSIMILATED GROUPS OR RADIATING CORES?

Here, inevitably, an important question arises: Why favor the gathering together of the local church instead of other kinds of gatherings of Christians? The Catholic Church in France has a wealth of different groups, movements, and charities: prayer groups, groups for reflection, missionary action groups and groups devoted to charitable or liturgical work. Wouldn't it make a lot of sense to make use of these groups to reconstruct a new kind of parish? One no longer territorial, but located where all these groups merge like rivers running into each other, with the help of an ordained minister who could coordinate them and with the help of the Eucharist which makes them exist as church?

But there is a fundamental difference, and even a difference in nature, between groups of Christians and a local church. The existence and the life of a group, or movement, depends on members of the group assimilating other members into the group, inspired by a commonly agreed-upon objective; the sanctification of the members, works of service for the church, charitable works, etc. The local church, on the other hand, gathers in a public place, known by everyone and accessible to all. It is localized but not territorial in the sense that those who come to it can come from anywhere, even if a core of regulars is necessary for the life of this community. The essential characteristic is what St. Paul talked about: "There is neither Jew nor Greek, there is neither slave nor free person, there is not male and female; for all are one in Christ Jesus" (Galatians 3:28). This is not a process of assimilation. We welcome each other in the name of the Lord; whatever we are and wherever we come from, whatever our place of origin, culture, age, sex, personal history, or degree of integration into the Christian faith. We welcome them because they have heard the call. It is an open assembly.

This characteristic remains the one that carries the strongest meaning of the universality of the Christian message and of the catholicity of the church, as much for those outside as for those within.

> *The more the churches are dispersed,*
> *the more welcoming they need to become,*
> *and the more they need to keep in communion*
> *with the other churches.*

CHAPTER 4

CHRISTIAN INITIATION

*"What you have come to
is the assembly of the firstborn"*

cf. Hebrews 12:23

Less spectacular than the drop in the number of Mass attendants and priests in active ministry (but perhaps of greater significance) are the changes that have affected Christian baptism in French catholicism. At the same time that the percentage of infant baptisms has dropped dramatically, the number of adult catechumens has gone from a few dozen to several thousand.*

We could consider this phenomenon decisive in the transition from a Christian society (where baptism was part of one's civil identity) to a secular society (in which religious adherence is the fruit of a personal decision that implies a certain way of life). Anyone today who wants to resolutely follow the gospel must make a clear break with certain customs of the surrounding society. The revaluing of what baptism signifies and the lifestyle of the baptized act as conditioners for the vitality and the witness of local churches dispersed in a secular world.

DEVALUED BAPTISM

While letting God be the judge of their hearts, we can state objectively that for a great number of our contemporaries, baptism as a Catholic has been a part of their basic integration into society. For some, baptism has apparently had no consequences for their lives. For others, perhaps more numerous, it goes hand in hand with the affirmation, "Yes, I'm a believer." But this profession of faith often denotes a remote and nebulous God, scarcely illuminated by biblical revelation.

---

* This is equally true in large sectors of the English-speaking world. — Editor

Jesus, Messiah, Son of God, and Redeemer remains a totally blurred figure, and this state of mind of the baptized is almost completely without any living relationship to the church.

In these conditions, Christian baptism is devalued. "This doesn't commit us to anything!" I have often heard from the mouths of parents asking for baptism for their baby. "Of course, he'll do what he wants later on."

Let us listen again to John Paul II in the encyclical already mentioned:

It is true that in some places sociological considerations associated with Baptism obscure its genuine meaning as an act of faith. This is due to a variety of historical and cultural factors that must be removed where they still exist, so that the sacrament of spiritual rebirth can be seen for what it truly is. Local ecclesial communities must devote themselves to this task.[10]

This is a powerful call that contrasts with the small effort that the ecclesiastical authorities have expended up to now to bring about a change in the situation. When I became pastor of a parish, I was told, "Except in the case of an explicit declaration of non-faith on the part of both parents at the same time, we do not refuse infant baptism." This direction was given despite the prescription of the *Code of Canon Law*, which attaches a condition to infant baptism: that there should be "a founded hope that the infant will be brought up in the Catholic religion."[11] Statistically, the lack of follow-up to baptism shows that in the vast majority of cases, this "founded hope" is wanting. But because in any particular case, "one is never sure what the future will bring," you baptize.

CONVERSION AND BAPTISM

When the witnesses of the Pentecost miracle asked Peter, "What are we to do?" he replied: "Repent, and be baptized, every one of you, in the name of Jesus Christ." You must change your lives: "Save yourselves from this corrupt generation!" (Acts of the Apostles 2:38-40).

Some people, especially young people, who have already been baptized as Catholics are attracted by the vigor of evangelical preachers who insist on conversion in order to follow Christ. They are told "Your baptism isn't worth anything since you had not first been converted." And so they have themselves rebaptized. Thus we are challenged by the lack of coherence between a sacrament

---

10 *Redemptoris Missio* 47.

11 *Code of Canon Law: Latin-English Edition* (Washington D.C.: Canon Law Society of America, 1983), canon 868.2.

that is supposed to be a sign of a new life and a lifestyle that does not signify faith in the gospel at all. Is what we once tolerated in a Christian society still acceptable in a *diaspora* church?

CHRISTIAN INITIATION

With an increasing demand for adult baptism, and with the progressive rediscovery of the catechumenal process, don't we have here one element of a reply to those who question the value of the profession of Christian faith? The necessity of restoring the catechumenate appeared clearly in France at the time of Vatican II and this perception deepened with the preparation of a new Rite of Christian Initiation of Adults. Now, with the vastly increased numbers of catechumens, it is seen as being even more necessary.

THE CATECHUMENATE: A SPECIAL PATHWAY

In order to restore a true catechumenate, it is not enough just to assure that the truths of faith are passed on and that several rites are celebrated in preparation for baptism. Christian initiation is a vital whole that provides an *entrée* into the faith and life of the church. Catechesis forms part of it, but it can never be separated from the sacramental rites or from the welcome within the believing community.

A JOURNEY WITH THE COMMUNITY

Of the three inseparable strands that are woven to make up Christian initiation (teaching, rites, community) the third is the most tenuous. Rare are those parishes and assemblies that feel themselves to be really *pregnant* with Christians in the process of gestation, whose new life can only be a life in the church. Rare are those places that give catechumens a special place in their liturgies; for example, during the Sunday scrutinies in the season of Lent that precedes their baptism. Rare are those that forge real human, affectionate and warm ties with the catechumens in their journey of conversion and their apprenticeship to prayer. Rare are those who have understood that the Liturgy of the Word in Sunday assemblies, in which the catechumens have the right to take part, ought to take into account their capacity to listen and their participation in the songs and prayers, even though they cannot yet share at the eucharistic table. And all this presupposes that Sunday assemblies are not made up solely of practicing members who come to *get their Mass,* but in fact become true ecclesial base communities.

THE RITES OF INITIATION

This second strand of the catechumenal cord is still largely to be rediscovered and to be reinvented as far as forms are concerned. The rites of the catechumenate are not merely ceremonies that have to take place before baptism, they are already the beginning of the sacrament itself. Word and sacrament are inextricably linked, you cannot separate the two.

In comparison with the richness of the catechumenal stages of the early church, our stages are very poor at a symbolic level. There are several reasons for this. There was a break in the transmission of the living tradition of the stages on the way to baptism. Moreover, a rationalist, Cartesian and scientific mentality is scarcely oriented toward ritual symbols and their mystagogy.

Among the cultural shifts taking place today is a rebirth of the symbolic, which provides a favorable context for a new liturgical inculturation. The period of catechumenate is already a special *locus* for the inculturation of faith, and will be so increasingly in the future.

A KIND OF AUTO-INCULTURATION

For there to be symbol, there must be culture, but at the present time we are witnessing a fragmentation of culture and of cultures. Symbolization is based on a common sharing by people. A certain symbolic and figurative ensemble of biblical faith and Christian rites exists, but these rites themselves have been fragmented and appear to be more anecdotal than anything else.

As happened in the first centuries of Christianity we have been required to make an autoinculturation of the rites in our local churches. This process presupposes experience and discernment; it is work that will take a long time to achieve. The new RCIA foresaw this.[12]

This task is a matter of urgency. We need initiation rites adapted to the different stages of the catechumenal journey. We need to find ways to make use once more of the only form of baptism that carries the full meaning of the sacrament which is immersion, descent into the waters and rising out of them. We need to rediscover a perfumed anointing of the whole body, which will also bathe with its scent the eucharistic assembly where the neophytes are welcomed. We need chants that will stay with us for the rest of our lives as a memory of this night of grace, like those once sung by Asterius of Amasea in the era of the great paschal baptismal nights:

---

[12] *RCIA* 32ff.

O nuptial night of the Church

which brought to birth the newly baptized

and disarmed the sleeping demon!

O night when the Heir introduced

the heirs into their inheritance....

In the same way that the imminent
        birth of the baby is the primary concern
of its parents and its brothers and sisters,
so the arrival of a new Christian into the life
        of a local community
is for them a great grace-filled moment.

CHAPTER 5

THE CELEBRATING ASSEMBLY

*"The parts of the body, though many,
are one body"*

I Corinthians 12:12

According to the comparison that the apostle Paul makes between the local church and the human body, all the members are different and each one has its own function in the one body. Lest we forget, he reminds us that the most vulnerable or intimate parts are the ones that are treated with the greatest care.

For his part, James, in his letter, tells us to beware of any difference of treatment that we might make in the assembly between a dignitary and any other participant:

My brothers, show no partiality as you adhere to the faith in our glorious Lord Jesus Christ. For if a man with gold rings on his fingers and in fine clothes comes into your assembly, and a poor person in shabby clothes also comes in, and you pay attention to the one wearing the fine clothes and say, "Sit here, please," while you say to the poor one, "Stand there," or "Sit at my feet," have you not made distinctions among yourselves and become judges with evil designs? (James 2:1-4)

We need to look again at this question of the relationship between the members of the assembly in the liturgy. It is an important element in the current transition between a strongly hierarchical church and a church of communion in which all the baptized must be acknowledged as such in their differences and at the same time in their equal dignity.

CONCENTRATION ON THE PRIEST

We have already called to mind that in the early church there is evidence of a great variety of service, functions and ministries in local communities. From the beginning of what we call the Middle Ages onward, we see these ministries of service gradually becoming more and more feeble and concentrated in the ministry of the priest. There are many reasons for this historical evolution.

When the practice of the catechumenate died out around the 6th century, there was no further need for doorkeepers, exorcists, catechists, etc. When the faithful stopped receiving Communion at Sunday Mass, there was no further need for acolytes to take Communion to the sick and housebound. When the bishop became the major administrator of his diocese, he no longer needed deacons at his side to fulfill this task.

Thus it was that priests progressively became invested with all the pastoral tasks in the new parishes, and in a more and more exclusive manner as regards worship and the sacraments.

IN A CLASS SOCIETY

In a highly structured class society, alongside the lords who defended their territory and the serfs who worked the land, the cleric was at the same time a man of knowledge and a man of the sacred.

Today, we are just emerging from the period where the structure of society projected its image on the gatherings of the church.* In the village church of my childhood, we still had the Palace Pew for the local nobility, the Churchwardens' Pew for the parish dignitaries, rented pews in a hierarchy according to price, and finally the seats for "the others."

CLASSES IN WORSHIP

Other kinds of structure affected the sacred rather more closely. There was a very visible and very strict separation between the sanctuary and the nave. The sanctuary, demarcated by a closed grille, was reserved to members of the clergy or those who had been assimilated into this class, cantors, sacristans, choristers, all necessarily of the male sex. Beyond the sanctuary were the others....

Certain clerical or sex-based barriers have been partially dismantled, but it would be a mistake to dream of the disappearance of all differences. If each

---

*The discussions in the United States surrounding the use of the national flag in churches following the events of September 11, 2001, showed that such structures are still to be found. — Editor

person has received a different gift for the good of all, how will this gift become known? And if every person who has a public role in the assembly necessarily exercises his personal power there, how can the assembly "manage" this person?

If the manifestation of differences originating in the world is incongruous in the Christian assembly, the same cannot be said of the differences arising from the diversity of the gifts of the Spirit, differences that manifest the richness of the ecclesial body. We will need to return to this question.

THE WAY THE ASSEMBLY PERCEIVES ITSELF

For those who are gathered in the name of the Lord, the image they have of their visible congregation necessarily influences their state of mind and their behavior. Thus the number of people and the way they are arranged in the space have an effect on the celebration and an impact on its meaning.

A group of only a few dozen people can more easily recognize and welcome the gifts that God has given to certain members for the good of the whole body. The more the number of participants increases, the more those with something to do become anonymous and the more their role appears to be purely functional. We quickly and almost inevitably reach the stage of distinguishing two categories of people: on the one hand, the active members who emerge from the ranks of the assembly and constitute the ministers, and on the other hand, the passive members who receive.

DIMENSIONS OF THE ASSEMBLY

Some historians think that Christian assemblies in the early centuries, which took place in houses capable of accommodating them, numbered no more than a few dozen people on average. The majority of Romanesque churches in rural French parishes, as well as the cave churches of Cappadocia, presuppose assemblies roughly comparable in size.

In certain centers of population, large churches were built from the 4th century onward and, during the Middle Ages, cathedrals and shrines for pilgrimage were constructed. Initially these were places for gathering around the person of the bishop, or gathering at a hallowed spot, and not the place where the ordinary worship of the local churches took place. It seems that the growth in size of parish churches in certain regions coincided with the success of parish missions during the 17th and 18th centuries and the population growth of the 19th century.

FROM ASSEMBLY TO WORSHIP SPACE

The question of the optimum size of ordinary local assemblies is very important to us today because of the change of style in liturgical celebrations and, in some places, the large decrease in the numbers of those attending.

When considering the place for our assembly, we should not use the buildings we have inherited as a starting point. Quite the contrary, the place must be chosen or arranged as a function of the size of the assemblies in such a way that the interactions among the participants can assume their full human, symbolic, and sacramental significance.

We will always need large churches for big gatherings, especially liturgies presided over by the bishop: baptisms at the Easter Vigil (and other baptismal days that are already being talked about), confirmations, ordinations, etc., as well as for all kinds of regional events such as festival Eucharists, different sorts of gatherings, etc.

At the other end of the scale, optional groups such as prayer groups, Bible study groups, groups for reflection or formation, etc., will all select venues that suit them.

THE SUNDAY ASSEMBLY

However, in the situation of a scattered church in which we find ourselves, the Sunday assembly, the foundational sign of the church, which must be at once open to all and very human while at the same time being very prayerful and very sacred, both very fraternal and very mystical, runs the risk of becoming depersonalized and banal if it always consists of a large number of participants on ordinary Sundays.

In the churches where I celebrated frequently, I knew exactly at which pew in the nave direct communication ceased, communication by gesture, look, or voice. Beyond that point, what was expressed became unclear or mechanized. We have created a huge gulf through the microphones and loudspeakers that have enslaved us. So I say, "Long live small churches!"

The act of Communion in particular, that sacramental summit of the Mass, in large assemblies is in danger of losing its meaning of all sharing at the same table, becoming instead a large number of separate consumptions. We need to reflect on the difference between the multiplication of the loaves for the crowds and the Last Supper with the disciples.

Another determining factor is the way in which the assembly is laid out. The assembly must be able to see itself as an assembly that listens to the same Word, that sings the same song, that prays the same intentions. From this comes a preference for an enveloping layout that is beginning to arouse serious interest, i.e., an assembly where there also exists lateral communication, even if it is diffuse.

THE POWER OF THOSE WHO DO SOMETHING

When members of the assembly do something at the service of the assembly, those persons necessarily exercise a sort of power over the assembly. When they speak to the assembly or are silent, when they sing verses or silently carry an object, what they do is neither for themselves alone nor like a ceremonial functionary, but as a servant of God and humankind, so those who are watching can feel themselves touched. Everything is happening as if they themselves were carrying out this ministry, and thus all are placed in a certain relationship with God.

We can see three levels in this synergy. The first is the level of *sensitivity*; are they doing it from their place or from a special place? Are they turned toward the assembly to read, but toward Christ at the moment of common prayer? The second level is *functional*; are they reading passages taken from the Lectionary, or offering spontaneous intentions for prayer? The third is the level of *mystery*; in whose name are they intervening, in their own or in the name of the group? Are they doing so because of their acknowledged competence or because they have been designated to do so by someone in charge? Or was it by virtue of sacramental ordination? These questions, whether implicit or explicit, cannot be avoided in liturgical celebration.

CORRESPONDING TO THEIR ROLE

If not everything always needs to be manifested in ritual roles, in general it is necessary for authority exercised in a ritual manner to be done for the cohesion and peace of the group. Since the reforms of Vatican II, we have often been forced to remain in a state of some fluidity regarding acts of service and the ministers who fulfill them. We needed to reinvent them, while at the same time having only a limited space to maneuver within the laws currently in force. We must not forget that we are not very far removed from a time when only the priest had the right to do what a layperson did not have the right to do, a time when men were allowed to fulfill certain roles but women were not. The proper place for ministers will only become clear when the whole assembly is the primary subject and celebrant.

THE BAPTIZED, SUBJECTS OF THE CELEBRATION AND ACTORS IN IT

At the moment of anointing the newly baptized
   with holy chrism, the priest says:

[God] now anoints you with the chrism of salvation

so that, united with his people,

you may remain for ever a member of Christ

who is Priest, Prophet, and King.

And we remind those to be confirmed that, "you have become members of Christ and of his priestly people."[13] We often use a song that begins, "Priestly people, kingly people...."[14]

This kind of language, rooted in the Bible, is often difficult for the faithful to understand. They ask "How can we be priests when only priests can say Mass and give absolution?" or "What does the expression 'priestly people' mean? Is it all the clergy?"

It is not easy to undo the traditional understanding of the words *priest* and *priesthood*, but it is nevertheless necessary in order to appreciate the idea and the reality of the baptismal priesthood desired by Vatican II. This goes to the very heart of the concept of Christian life and liturgical action, for the question here is of the priesthood *par excellence*, which is that of Christ and of the church.

We must also not forget that we use the word *priest* in two different senses, a general sense to indicate those who offered sacrifice and ministered in pagan religions and in the Temple at Jerusalem and a Christian sense which is denoted by the Latin word *presbyter* or elder. It is one of the first ministries to appear in the early church, after the apostles and evangelists. It is not individual but collegial. Every local church needs to be provided with this kind of priesthood.

Now we can better understand this extract from the General Instruction on the Roman Missal of Paul VI:

---

13 *RCIA* 228, 233.

14 By Fr. Lucien Deiss. The English version will be found in *Biblical Hymns and Psalms vol. I*, # 34, published by World Library, 1966.

In the celebration of Mass the faithful constitute a holy people, a people God has made his own, a royal priesthood: they give thanks to the Father and offer the victim not only through the hands of the priest but also together with him and learn to offer themselves.[15]

All offer and all are offered. The manner of celebrating must signify this, as we will see especially in the case of the eucharistic prayer. But in a general way the baptized continue to think "It's the priest who does the Mass; we just attend it." Or, as I have often heard during preparation with families for a baptism or a funeral, "Oh Father, you know what to do; we don't." This is true of the rites themselves, but not for the essence of the action by a believer.

There is no reason to fear, as one sometimes hears, that the rediscovery by the laity of the priesthood of their baptism could adversely affect the proper nature of the ordained minister called the "ministerial priesthood." There are even good grounds for thinking exactly the opposite.

ASSEMBLIES AND COMMUNITY

If the celebration needs acts of service and ministries, these do not exhaust the varied gifts distributed by the Spirit for the life of the local church, in particular the proclamation of the gospel, the life of fellowship, sharing with the poor, and giving help to the mentally and physically sick. That is to say, we should not equate the assembly, liturgical or not, with the community of Christians in a local church.

Every assembly is transitory. It takes place in a given place at a given time, with particular participants. Then it dissolves away. There are never two identical assemblies, so each assembly is a unique event.

The community is stable, at least in part. It includes all the baptized and catechumens of a local church, even if all of these are not present at all the assemblies in that place. It includes one or more core groups that, among others, prepare and support the assemblies that take place. The community possesses the assemblies.

Inversely, the assembly fashions the community through prayer, the word, and the sacraments. The assembly is ceaselessly reminded that it is not fully Christian and not yet the kingdom of God, but that its task is to prepare for the coming of that kingdom.

---

[15] GIRM 62.

THE CONTRIBUTION OF THE MONKS

Monastic charism is essential to the life of the church, celibacy to signify waiting for the coming of the Bridegroom, continual prayer which makes incarnate vigilance for the return of the Master, and detachment from the goods of this world with a view to the world that is to come and for the purpose of sharing between human brothers and sisters. All this is at the heart of the gospel and needs to be manifested in local communities.

When I was preparing my thesis on psalmody in the Syrian churches of the 4th and 5th centuries, I discovered to my astonishment that the first people to arrive at the Sunday assembly were the monks. They were men and women from widely differing backgrounds, living alone or in community. They began to sing and to pray while the people were arriving and those people would gradually join in with their praying and singing, right up until the arrival of the various ministers for the Liturgies of the Word and the Eucharist. These monks or ascetics did not take on particular liturgical functions. They safeguarded the gift of living prayer in the midst of the people.

From the 6th century on, the active participation of the faithful diminished in the assemblies and, since the monks wanted to distance themselves from the rest of the church within a Christian society, parishes and monasteries no longer coincided at the Sunday Eucharist.

How many times on a Sunday morning, arriving in the little assemblies in my area where a few of the faithful courageously made sure that the celebration of Mass would take place, have I said to myself, "If only men and women of prayer were with us!" In a church that is becoming more and more scattered, how the church's assemblies are in need of such a presence at their Sunday Eucharist! The liturgy proper to monks is the daily sanctification of the hours, but the Sunday Eucharist is the liturgy of the local church of which all the baptized are part.

The more actively each member plays his or her part,
the more alive the body will be.

CHAPTER 6

PRAYERS—WORD—MEAL

The seed in a receptive heart.

Cf. Luke 8:15

We have just been reminding ourselves how, at the period when on the Lord's Day a single Eucharist would gather the members of the local church, the celebration did not begin immediately with the reading of scripture but with a fairly long time of prayers during which all could settle themselves comfortably.

The specific mention of *the prayers*, alongside the teaching of the Apostles and the breaking of bread in the description that Luke gives us of the first Christian community in Jerusalem, is certainly there for a purpose. The current context of our Sunday assemblies can help us to understand it.

THE BASIS OF TAKING STEPS FORWARD IN RELIGION

We could say that there is a true religious act taking place from the very moment when people address the divinity from the bottom of their hearts, by adding, or not, a ritual act to their word, or to their silence.

It is interesting to observe how, in our secularized world where a large number of children and young adults have practically no experience of prayer, the awakening or reawakening of a religious sense, opening up to transcendence and to the sacred, is most often aroused by a living encounter with an act of prayer: a monastic choir chanting the office, a prayer group alternating words, chants and silences, a person in an unmoving and prayerful posture, or even a period of silence during a baptism or a wedding. The important thing is not what is said or done but the act of prayer itself, perceived as such.

PRAYERFUL HOSPITALITY

This statement suggests a question. Isn't the assembly at prayer the pathway to and preferred *locus* of Christians' hospitality in faith? Is it not for the one who has a clear desire for God and for those who do not know what they are seeking, for the one who already has some adherence to a religion and for those who do not? Prayer can touch those who practice their faith and those who do not, catechumens and inquirers, those who are anchored in a specific faith community and those who are not.

Does the local ecclesial community offer this kind of hospitality, not only in prayer groups or prayer communities, but also in public places open to all and easily accessible? And in France what could be closer at hand for that than the churches of our towns and villages whose doors can be pushed open by anyone? And isn't the Sunday assembly the first opportunity to offer hospitality in faith?

ENTERING INTO PRAYER

The ceremonial of the Roman Mass certainly includes opening rites that are intended to help those arriving "to listen to God's word and celebrate the Eucharist properly."[16] But are these rites suitable for the purpose of inciting those who have crossed the threshold to enter into adoration, the fundamental expression of all genuine prayer?

The post-Vatican II Mass was conceived in terms of assemblies of Western Catholic Christians, baptized believers, duly catechized and initiated into the sacraments of the church. Such assemblies do undoubtedly exist, thanks be to God, but the most common reality is different. We often find ourselves in the presence of assemblies consisting increasingly of baptized people who have never received catechesis, along with catechumens and inquirers. The majority of them are not very familiar with our rites and what we sing and they know even less about the Bible.

Faced with these situations, our present introductory rites appear to be both overloaded and too short, overloaded with words and songs and lacking in silence and prayer of adoration. The penitential rite, for example, comes too soon. You need to have heard and welcomed the word of salvation in order to "turn yourself around" and recognize yourself as a sinner before God. The opening prayer (collect) goes by too quickly, without a suitable context, and acts of praise and supplication do not have enough time to affect the inner being.

---

[16] GIRM 24.

A TIME FOR PRAYER

What happens in my community? When someone enters the church, prayer is already happening. A group of people around a lamp, an icon, a bouquet of flowers, the cross or the Bible are humming, murmuring psalms, leading litanies, offering some intentions for prayer punctuated with silence. Visitors will find a place within this activity. One might walk out again, for he didn't come in to pray; perhaps another will remain at the back of the church to see what happens; perhaps one will sit down to recollect; yet another might come and join the group. The call is being issued to each person's deep-seated freedom. It is to one's desire that the call is sent, without which no symbol will have meaning and no word will speak to the heart.

At the end of quite a long period of time, maybe at the official starting for the liturgy of the day, the book of the scriptures is brought in and acclaimed. All those who wish to do so now follow it and gather themselves around the ambo.

A TIME FOR THE WORD

We know this only too well. Everything flows from the revealed word that will be read, explained, meditated upon, given back in praise and supplication to the one who addresses the word to us. All of this is familiar to us. But what is the right proportion for each of these elements?

The quantity and choice of the biblical readings that will be read depend on how much fruit we believe they will bear in those who will hear them. This is because the rites do not exist for themselves and they do not give glory to God except through the human beings that are sanctified by them. We still need to remind ourselves of this, even after Vatican II, for ritualism incessantly rears its ugly head.

The choice and the ordering of the readings provided by the *Lectionary for Sunday Mass* constitute a remarkable treasure and give rich nourishment. Nevertheless, it is necessary in every individual case to ask if the quantity, and sometimes the choice, of the texts offered actually correspond to the ability of the listeners to assimilate them. Too many texts read out, but not understood and not explained, can overwhelm and engender fatigue and disinterest.

Even if we can joyfully note a continued increase in quality in the way the readings are carried out in our assemblies, it still happens all too often that the readings are read too quickly and in a boring, humdrum tone. On the other hand, and this is encountered even more frequently, the homilist either presupposes too much knowledge on the part of the listeners or else wanders away from the text in generalities, without having really explained the biblical meaning of the words and expressions, the symbolism of the narratives, or the state of mind of the persons mentioned in such a way that each listener, even someone completely uneducated, can feel called upon by the word and taken up into the story in which each will discover who he or she really is.

A TIME FOR RESPONDING

The way of the word should not stop once the meaning of words and things has been understood intellectually. The word needs to descend from the head into the heart, and touch it so that it may be turned around in the direction of the Spirit in order to be nourished and comforted by the Spirit, so that the word can then pass from the heart to the hands.

For this to happen, a time for ruminating on the word is necessary. The psalm certainly fulfills this function, especially if each person is engaged in savoring the words of the poem in a collective, slow and meditative act of psalmody. The poem is spoken in a rhythm and there is a pause at the end of each line to give time for an inner echoing. True psalmody interiorizes. The psalm suffuses the whole celebration with peace and silence. And, contrary to what is generally believed, it is very easy and very beneficial to have psalmody prayed by everyone.

In every age, the church has also responded to the word by means of hymns, according to the language, culture, and piety of the period and place. In the Middle Ages, the number of chants between the readings was multiplied with tracts and sequences. The Mass we have today does not envisage this kind of popular hymnody as such, but neither does it exclude it. All kinds of proposals have been put forward for the Liturgy of the Word, with the aim of restoring a balance between the word proclaimed and the precious part that a lyrical response has to play as we see in the Eastern liturgies or in the old Latin Mass. These suggestions have not been successful. "We haven't got time." It is said, "There are already too many things to do and say." Surely, we need to take a fresh look at the proportion of time allocated to words, readings and commentaries, the time for active assimilation of those words and those times of silence and inner listening which should not be lacking, in order that all of these may be as fruitful as possible.

A TIME FOR ASKING

Nourished by the liberating word, the whole assembly can cry out to God, "All that you have declared and promised, do it now for your people and for the world." It is the time of supplication and intercession, a moment so fittingly named universal prayer[17] where we open up our hearts to the dimension of the whole church, of humanity, of the world and history, until the kingdom comes. People cried out *"Maranatha!"* at this point in ancient Christian liturgies.

We should note that at one time the Our Father was said in this part of the rite, a good place for it, coming as it does before the time when those who cannot participate in the breaking of the bread leave the assembly of prayer and word.

AROUND THE TABLE

At this point, those who have been fully introduced into the mystery of the body of the Lord regroup themselves around the table at which the Lord invites us to live his *Pasch* with him. Those who are on the way toward full communion and who have not yet reached that stage, as is the case in assemblies that welcome catechumens, are allowed to withdraw before the eucharistic meal. This is not done out of contempt or a sense of exclusivity, but out of respect and truthfulness. And it is also out of respect and truthfulness that the only ones who remain to eat and drink are those who can recognize the body of the Lord[18] in the sacrament and in the church that celebrates it.

ECUMENICAL HOPE

The greatest scandal of Christians is their non-communion and their divisions. How can those to whom the Master said, "This is how all will know that you are my disciples, if you have love for one another" (John 13:35) refuse to take the first step toward unity which is praying together, that is to say, praying together to our common Father, together imploring the Father's mercy and forgiveness, confessing the same faith in the same hope?

Thank God, many barriers have already fallen down and others continue to fall. High-level doctrinal agreements have been reached and mistrust has disappeared between neighbors. But as long as people continue to go to *their* church or *their* temple or *their* assembly, as long as they pass by the homes of others

---

[17] In Latin, *oratio universalis*. In English, we also have the U.S. usage "prayers of the faithful" and the English usage "bidding prayers," but the expression "general [i.e., global] intercessions" comes closest to expressing what is contained in the Latin. — Translator

[18] Cf. 1 Corinthians 11:29

without going in to take the primary step, to pray together to the same Lord, the ecumenical movement will remain blocked.

What is it, then, that keeps us from praying together and letting ourselves be challenged by the same word? What keeps us from offering prayers of supplication together for the coming of the kingdom? What do Christians find so difficult in this, as we wait for the time when we can in complete peace and utter clarity share the same bread and drink the same cup?

This decisive ecumenical advance will not be achieved by decrees from on high. It will depend on the opening of our local assemblies. It is by this sign, visible to everybody, that the Good News that we announce will be rendered credible for all those who live around us.

> *God has already answered the prayer*
> *of those who have come to an agreement*
> *to petition God together.*

CHAPTER 7

RITES AND BODIES

*"Offer your bodies as a living sacrifice,
holy and pleasing to God..."*

Romans 12:1

This is really what St. Paul wrote to the Romans, even if many translators, perhaps fearful of a double meaning, paraphrase Paul's words as "Offer your persons" or "Offer yourselves" or "Offer your lives" — all of which hold the body at a distance. Nevertheless, we have strong human expressions such as "to risk your neck" or "to feel it in your guts" which do not shy away from the body. Because the heart of the gospel is the giving up of life, and because the nub of our faith is the resurrection of the *body*, the body is certainly the very *locus* of our spiritual sacrifice to God, as it was for Jesus who offered himself "in his flesh."[19]

LITURGY AND BODY

A fortiori, when it is a question of liturgy, everything happens through our bodies; word, singing, music, light, scent, anointing, bathing, bread and wine. Everything reaches us via our senses. And our response passes via our mouth, our voice, our hands, our feet and the whole of our body.

It is very obvious to say this, but not at all obvious to practice it. I come from a generation where good manners required rigorous control of anything that had to do with the body: modesty and restraint, endurance and self-mastery, control of spontaneous reactions, tears and bursts of laughter. The least excess was considered indecent.

---

[19] Cf. Romans 8:3, 1 Timothy 3:16.

In prayer, whether personal or communal, behavior often comes down to a kneeling posture, with upright and unmoving torso, hands joined with fingers interlaced and eyes closed. But what can be good for certain forms of personal meditation is not necessarily consistent with liturgy.

THE BODY HELD AT ARM'S LENGTH

In the 1950s, when the first tremors of a renewal in the participation of the faithful in the liturgy were just starting to impinge on certain parish assemblies, I was in the brand new *Institut Supérieur de Pastorale Catéchétique* (Advanced Institute of Pastoral Catechetics) of the *Institut Catholique* (Catholic Institute) in Paris teaching religious symbolism. I was not teaching liturgy because that word could only be used for rubrics inscribed in the official books and for the Latin language. I searched out the Director, F. Coudreau, and said to him, "How can I initiate into the art of celebration all these priests and nuns who pray as if they had no bodies! What we need first of all are workshops in bodily expression." Permission was granted, but then the enterprise was denounced to Pope Pius XII himself because "priests and female religious are turning their attention to their bodies — together!"

THE BODY EMBRACED

From the point of view of the surrounding culture, things have moved on a lot since that time. A liberation of the body has taken place in the domains of dress, behavior, intermingling of the sexes, the development of sport, etc. If social control has lost some of its values in this area, the liturgical renewal has in part gained from it, especially in the domains of singing and postures for prayer. Among young people in general, and especially in certain prayer groups, people now feel much freer to pray sitting back on their heels, prostrate, or with hands raised, swaying their bodies back and forth or clapping their hands. Evidently children, who are not so self-conscious as their elders, show themselves to be very spontaneous in their participation in processions, rhythmic actions, songs, etc.

PARALYZED ASSEMBLIES

And yet the spectacle that the assemblies in our churches most often present us with is a paralyzed assembly. First of all, people are trapped within rows of chairs or between pews. No one moves except to go to Communion. Between arriving and departing, you stand up or you sit down. That's all. There is no gesture of adoration at the beginning, nor any bowing to ask pardon before receiving the body of Christ. Sometimes a few scattered hands are raised at the Our Father.

The important thing here is not the demonstration of bodily participation. Europeans don't have to copy African dances. But a serious loss of intensity and human truth occurs if the Spirit has no other pathways to act than through our eyes and our ears. What is an acclamation if the whole of one's being is not invested in it? What is psalmody if all our inner beings do not swing back and forth with the parallelism of the couplets? What are our hands if they never move to implore or to praise?

EACH ACTOR HAS HIS OWN ROLE

The role of the body in liturgy is particularly important for all those who fulfill a ritual function in the liturgy. It is not very often that we find a presiding minister, or a lector, or someone carrying an object, or someone in procession who is taking on his role to the fullest. Many people instinctively and unconsciously conceal their individuality, which is the opposite of their role.

Here, too, we need to offer our bodies in the rite, offer them to the action of the Spirit for the good of the assembled church. Role and personality are in no way in opposition to each other. Isn't a person there precisely for the other person? In this way we have been able to remind ourselves of the importance of vestments in all liturgical roles. The service garb is also one way of offering one's body.

A BODY FOR THE SPIRIT

The offering of one's body in the liturgy is not carnal in the sense that it would be if we were talking about a physical action with a sensual or erotic end in view. It needs to be only, but fully, human, conscious, free, and spiritual.

Here we find the essential role of the word, always joined to the action through which it becomes sacrament. This word gives meaning and orientation at the same time as it gives the conditions and demands of truth, for worship that is pleasing to God involves our entire existence as an individual and social believer. The Gospel never ceases to remind us of this: "I was hungry...I was thirsty...naked...and you gave me...and you never gave me...." (Matthew 25:31-45).

IN THE MEANING WHICH COMES TO US

The rite is only a form perceivable by the senses, which evokes the invisible. It causes what it signifies. It does what it says. It is the summit of fullness: "Take and eat: this is my body, given up." But this effective word that causes the mystery also calls on another word: "What I have done, you must also do."

We need to pass from desire to concrete action. Nothing is more a part of our life than the sacramental rite. But the rite only has meaning if it is always anticipating the concrete gestures of our mortal condition.

The whole risen body derives from a completion that runs directly contrary to our time, like the new city and the new body descending from the heavens.

THE BODY AS PERFORMER

Looked at from the point of view of the ministers, the rite is a sort of performance. It's the same as with a musical score that an instrumentalist is playing.

Perhaps the instrumentalist correctly performs what is written down while remaining outside the work that is being performed, as if not involved in it. For the listener, the work sounds dead, unless the listener knows it well enough to recreate an ideal performance inside himself or herself, and happily this is possible.

Or perhaps the instrumentalist is so engaged in the work that he or she plays it as if it were his or her own piece, expressing through it his or her own emotions of sadness or joy, passion or amusement. But we are not there for the performer to give us his or her state of mind at any given moment.

Or again, the instrumentalist may hand over the whole of his or her being to the service of the work itself, giving each note its opportunity, sounding each chord in the best possible way so that each musical phrase takes on meaning. The purpose is not to impose on the listeners the performer's own emotions or his or her own interpretation. The purpose is for each person to receive, via the work, what he or she was waiting for without knowing it.

BODY — SACRAMENT

Such is the role of ministers of the word and of the sacraments; they are handling realities which are infinitely beyond them and which, by their nature, remain ungraspable. But they give each word and action its opportunity, letting themselves flow into those words and actions, without wanting to impose on their concelebrants what they are feeling or thinking at any given moment, but rather respecting what is actually taking place in the hearts of the participants.

Ministers must respect the ritual mystery and the mystery of the other person. In a fundamental sense, sacred ministers are performers. They are the intermediaries who place between the *sign/code* (Bible, sacrament, rite) and the public what is necessary so that the rite celebrated here and now might take on meaning and be efficacious. The sacrament passes between one body and another body, for the sake of the coming of the body.

But if ministers content themselves with doing what they have to do without investing any of themselves in it, or if, on the contrary, they try to impose their interpretation of a particular word or action, their bodies become a dam or a narrow strait at precisely the point where they ought to be opening the sluice gates for the living waters of the Spirit.

SEEDS IN ABUNDANCE

Seen from the point of view of the public, the rites are likes balls that are thrown to them, so numerous that they can only catch a few of them. But those that they do catch certainly seize them, perhaps because those particular balls are questioning them, or enlightening them, or upsetting them, or giving them courage.

THE SOWER OF THE GOSPEL SCATTERS SEED
IN ALL KINDS OF SOIL

But the capability of catching the balls or welcoming the seeds depends on the opening of the senses, the awakening of the spirit, the awaiting of desire where all can be engulfed in the breath of the Spirit.

Sacrificing one's own body begins there. It will be finally accomplished in the concrete actions of an existence that is completely given over by love, in the body offered by the only Son to his Father.

And for those who love, everything becomes grace.

Inasmuch as something of the body has not
been handed over,
the sacrifice cannot be perfect.

CHAPTER 8

INCULTURATION

"Each one heard them speaking in his own language."
Acts of the Apostles 2:6

Could there ever be a universal form of worship? A single liturgy for the whole world? No, no more than there could ever be a single language and a single culture for the whole of humanity.

Nevertheless, the question of the universality of Christian worship is one that has to be asked as soon as we recognize that the gospel message and Christian salvation are addressed to people of all times and all places. What has the church been doing since Pentecost?

First of all, we could note that none of the essential elements of Christian worship is proper to that form of worship alone. Its principal rites derive from all the most basic forms of human behavior which are at the same time the most rich in symbolic potential: the baptismal bath from the bathing of the newborn child to the washing of the body laid out for a funeral; the meal as an act essential to life, and an act that is indissolubly individual and social; the anointing of a body that has its own oils is like skincare which allows what is exterior to communicate with what is interior. Even the cross, before being linked to the death of the Savior and thus becoming the most specific sign of Christianity, is through its very configuration a universal symbol.

THE NECESSITY FOR INCULTURATION

To this first observation we could add a second. Christian rites, even the most central and foundational, have not been carried out in the same way as in the different times and places in which Jesus' followers first celebrated them. In the Latin church, baptism ceased to be a bath and became an ablution. For centuries the faithful did not share in the bread at Sunday Eucharist. The anointing of the whole body with perfumed oil was virtually abandoned. And yet, all these rites were held as valid and recognized as sacraments of the apostolic faith.

Every rite is necessarily inculturated and, through this, the incarnation of the word is prolonged. If a sign is not part of a culture and not part of the symbolic repertoire of a culture, it is no longer identifiable as a rite and can signify everything or nothing. Thus the rite of the pouring of water became scarcely identifiable any longer as a baptism unless there was a baby present. The first time I carried out the baptism of a child of school age at Mass in the parish of Villecerf, some people said afterwards, "But *that* wasn't a baptism!" The other side of the coin is that I find the African rites incomprehensible if someone does not explain them to me.

INDIGENOUS AND IMPORTED RITES

Christianity has always assumed that its rites could emigrate elsewhere. This is clear in the case of the language used. You can't proclaim the good news of the gospel except in a language understood by those you are talking to. Yet this did not prevent people from catechizing for hundreds of years in a vernacular language or dialect all the while continuing to celebrate the entire liturgy in Latin, right up to the day when the realization suddenly dawned that it didn't make sense to read the word of God without its message being understood by those for whom it was destined. The Reformers were able to benefit from the consequences of this realization. In the Catholic Church, we had to wait until the Second Vatican Council for a door in the liturgy to be opened up to every language, which could be a pathway allowing access to the message of faith.

Languages can be very diverse, but the word of God is one, like the faith of the church that proclaims that word.

MUSIC WITHOUT FRONTIERS?

One of the special areas for liturgical inculturation seems to be music. On the one hand, music crosses linguistic boundaries. In the parishes where I celebrated, we sang tunes from Ireland, Africa and China without anyone ever suspecting that they weren't "from round here." In the same way, when we sang certain medieval melodies such as Christmas carols, or airs from the time of the Renaissance such as Huguenot psalms, the young people did not perceive their origin. Making these chants their own was all that these assemblies had to do in order to appropriate them into their culture. It's the same thing with certain kinds of popular music broadcast in the media.

When I first arrived as pastor of Ville-Saint-Jacques, I found there a Society of St. Vincent of the Vine growers, despite the fact that there hadn't been any vines around for a long time! His feast was solemnly celebrated at the end of January each year. On this day, all the men — for once! — came to church, where they sang an astonishing "Hymn to St. Vincent," a *Kyrieleis* similar to the processional chants of the fifteenth century, preserved via oral tradition and unknown anywhere else. They all sang it at full volume in a particular style. It was starting from this element of the living tradition that I was able to reconstruct a contemporary liturgy of blessed bread offered to everyone and a local *chasselas* vine carried in procession by the "branch-bearers" of that year. This music, though both ancient and local, is still immediately accessible to children and to strangers.

If music can cross some frontiers it can at the same time signify with rare precision some of the peculiarities of a culture. At the same time we say, "That piece is by Mozart," Europeans in a particular way can also say, "That is our song." Each abbey, each community, group or parish has songs that make up part of its identity and which are exported as such. Conversely, the same words of the psalms of the Mass are used with different melodies. Inculturation did not impoverish the Christian message; rather it allowed us to discover its riches.

HOMEGROWN AND FROM ELSEWHERE

It is above all in bodily behavior that the inculturation of the rites is most easily recognizable. Muslims prostrate themselves to pray. An Orthodox Christian makes the sign of the cross backwards to our way of thinking. In Vietnam, the kiss of the altar in the Roman rite can have an immodest connotation. We could multiply examples *ad infinitum*.

Bodily behavior, though it can often seem almost imperceptible and done in an unconscious manner, is linked to a deeper sensitivity and to the way in which any given group lives together. This was the case for the act of genuflecting upon entering a church according to Catholic custom. One reason for this practice was to demonstrate a belief in the real presence in order to be distinguished from the Protestants.

Today, the majority of these special forms of group behavior have more or less disappeared. To some observers, it would seem that there are as many different liturgies, as many different ways in which celebrants behave, as many different sung repertoires, as many different ways of arranging people physically in a space (or even of taking the collection!) as there are parishes. But this impression is partly erroneous. There is a certain looseness in the rites because, as we came to the end of the twentieth century, Western culture itself had been somewhat damaged. In fact if there has been a casual, even negligent, attitude, it is also true that today we can sense a desire for new forms of coherence between mind and body, among individuals and groups and between one group and another. There is no evidence that we could find the models we need for Christian worship in what we rather simplistically term contemporary culture. It is rather in contemporary humanity, of which the media often present only the most superficial aspects, that we must look for the roots of the rites. It is in their celebrating assemblies that Christians must search for the optimum expressions of the revealed mysteries.

CHRISTIAN INITIATION IS THE STARTING POINT

New forms of coherence will appear in the faith of today's Christians when we have relearned and revalued the symbols of Christian initiation.

All the rites of initiation address the body with a view to its impregnation by the Spirit: *ephphetha*, the laying of hands, the public rejection of evil and profession of faith, bathing, anointing, the lighting of the baptismal candle, a new garment, approaching the table, the bread shared and the cup offered round.

It is true that most of our assemblies have a complete reconstruction job to do in the way in which they constitute themselves as assemblies in the church, in gestures of prayer in common, often non-existent, in the sharing in the Lord's Supper in a way that is both full of respect and of festivity, and so on. Often, we will look too far afield with means that are too sophisticated. If only we knew how to become like little children in the family of holy mother church.

THE ARTS, FREELY GIVEN AND YET ESSENTIAL

On a common anthropological background there appears the cultural bloom which is art, together with that freely given, and inexhaustible supplement, which we call beauty. All ritual practices in some way call on the various human arts.

The Australian aborigines do not have temples, but sacred places under the open sky in the desert where they gather for their festivals. With white eagle feathers they draw superb tapestries with mysterious graphic images in the soil. We know that when they were built, the interiors of our ancient Romanesque churches were covered with frescoes and paintings on vegetable, animal, biblical and sacramental themes.

Every historical period has invented such riches of meaning. Today, for example, floral arts are being increasingly used in celebration. After a period of considerable cleansing with raw stone reappearing, walls bare and white, we now see color returning. After the reign of the nonfigurative, figurative art is coming back again. After a time of liturgical vestments of conventional form, new forms are appearing.

The content of words is not sufficient: "Liturgical assemblies are searching for poets, musicians, painters, sculptors, architects…" not in order to create academies or museums, conservatories or experimental spaces, but because the living Spirit is multiform, just as from the very beginning the same Spirit has been multilingual.

FOREIGN LANGUAGE AND MOTHER TONGUE

No human form can enclose nor exhaust the Spirit, nor contradict nor destroy the Spirit. For the miracle of Pentecost is not to be found in the multitude of languages, a diversity which is as old as humanity itself and which is both a means of and a barrier to communication. The miracle is that "each one heard in his own native language"(Acts of the Apostles 2:8). Neither the diversity of cultures nor differences in ritual will ever be an obstacle to Christian worship: "Where the Spirit is, there is liberty," there is agreement, understanding, communion. Through the Spirit, any foreign language can become a mother tongue.

To look for symbols whose meaning would be universally acknowledged and understood in every culture, like the symbols used in mathematics or electronics, would be to reduce them to where they would be no more than signals with only one meaning. It should be the other way around. The more proverbs, myths, and sculptures are culturally determined, the better chance they have of unfolding meaning beyond the bounds of frontiers or centuries. Thus it is with the Bible, or with the person (actions and words) of Jesus, or with Christian rites in all their transformations across history. Our task is to hear them in our mother tongue.

A SLOW EVOLUTION

The miracle of Pentecost occurred only once. For us, the necessary inculturation of faith can only be a task for the long haul. Expected forms of evolution cannot be programmed, and, fortunately, they are not in the hands of a few reformers who know what has to be done and who can impose their will. For long centuries, in all the liturgical families, there have existed books which fixed the norms for celebration and handed down forms of ritual behavior. Yet people have always desired and sought out that which is most human in order that it may become that which is most transcendent.

As we have seen, deep cultural evolution is in progress and transformations are already at work in modes of ritual behavior. Everyone can very easily see what has disappeared: Latin, Gregorian chant, Roman ornaments, certain aspects of pontifical ceremonial, etc. But it is much more difficult to see what is being born. A wall falling to the ground makes much more noise than a seed growing in the ground. A certain emptiness, a certain hunger and a certain desire are all necessary if we are to achieve germination of these new seeds.

SHEDDING LIGHT ON THE RULES ALREADY IN FORCE

Some people have asked for a revision of the liturgical books that were refashioned after Vatican II, with a view to finding a place for new expectations for which we can now see the need: alternative formulas for certain prayers, a greater participation of the whole assembly (especially in the Eucharist), the lightening of a ritual structure that is still overburdened with words that don't have the time to speak properly and rites that don't have enough room for symbols to speak; an opening up to the values of art that are proper to each culture and to the current generation; and so on.

But is this the right pathway? To replace one regulation with another doesn't solve anything. The best law arises from usage that is recognized as good; law does not create good usage.

CONTINUED CREATIVITY

It is in the act of celebrating that we need to search out, try out, find out those things that can be proved to be a true support for the gospel and the action of the Holy Spirit. This presupposes a degree of flexibility and of innovation in the act of worship. We are talking about an art, not the execution of a technical program. We simultaneously need to know how to do it, to have a sense of the mystery and a flair for communication. I dare to say that I have made many liturgical discoveries in the very act of celebrating, both accidentally and also by making genuine mistakes in good faith.

RECEPTIVITY

It is over a period of time, by repeating a ritual form which appears to be a good one from one celebration to the next, that we can check its value. Generally speaking, the only decisive criterion of the relevance of a rite as far as action, symbol, melody or prayer-formula is concerned is whether it is *received.* In other words, when this repeated usage, like oil on water, spreads out from one assembly to another, and when the authorities, seeing its good effects, give tacit authorization to it. The great rites of the many different Christian liturgical families, in all their geographical and historical diversity, were originally put together through tacit recognition and adoption of models of how to do things that were recognized as being good.

HERE AND NOW

Each celebration is unique. Each celebration is always a re-creation. In order to be pastoral, each celebration is adapted to the assembly of the day, to the participants themselves, to the particular circumstances. It is in this act of service implied by the word *liturgy* itself, service that is attentive, watchful and fully pastoral, that we can discover little by little what is dead and moribund and what is alive and life-giving in the Spirit.

As a minister of worship, I toil and sow seeds. Certainly, only God gives the growth. But I am learning bit by bit in which soil and through which kinds of attention the seed will bear fruit. From one harvest to the next, good cultivation practices are refined.

The more a rite is inculturated in its form,
the more universally applicable will its message be.

Chapter 9

SINGING AND INSTRUMENTAL MUSIC

When you are together,
sing hymns, psalms and inspired songs in the Spirit.

Cf. Ephesians 5:18-19 and Colossians 3:16

In the 1950s, when we were looking for ways of satisfying the increasing expectations of French Catholics to be able to pray and sing in their mother tongue, a very cultivated person said to me, "You're going down completely the wrong pathway trying to get the faithful to sing in church. You're swimming against the current of contemporary culture. Today, French people themselves don't sing any longer, but they listen to beautiful music performed by those who know how to do it."

ASSEMBLIES THAT SING

Today, fifty years later, in the Catholic churches of France, people generally sing at Sunday Mass. In its own way, this is an extraordinary cultural revolution. Indeed, contemporary songs of all types are primarily sung by a singer and listened to on radio or disc, with the voice that reaches us usually supported by requisite rhythms and harmonies. This is a complete contrast with the kind of singing found in liturgical assemblies, which is collective by nature, most often in unison, and quite frequently without any instrumental accompaniment at all.

"IT'S UGLY"…"IT'S MAGNIFICENT"…

In certain professional musical circles, however, it is still good form to go around saying that "everything you hear in church is detestable." Moreover everybody knows, the nonprofessionals will add, that "the French are not musicians" and that "the French tongue isn't good for singing" as compared to Italian, or German, or English.

I want to state clearly and strongly that these statements are simply untrue. As a composer, I have had to write in a number of languages; the flexibility of the French language, in its approach to intensity, pitch, and duration, offers musicians an exceptional range of subtleties of expression. Duparc, Debussy, and many others have demonstrated the truth of this.

From a different point of view, as an average Frenchman, I do not find at the beginning of the twenty-first century that the French on the whole are especially deaf or indifferent to music. Indeed, having encouraged singing in many churches in my country, I can say that I find nothing that is more moving or more beautiful in its own way than an assembly singing in splendid unison with full voice, whether there are twenty people present or a thousand.

HYMNS AND SONGS

But that does not mean that I think there is nothing left to do, nothing left to discover and create in the area of liturgical singing, following the momentum of renewal set in motion by Vatican II, in order to achieve truth and beauty in the common sung prayer of our assemblies.

For the church was born singing. We see it clearly enough with the Colossians whom Paul encouraged (Colossians 3:16), in Bithynia according to Pliny the Younger, and we see it in Syria and in Egypt. The letter to the Ephesians, rather in the style of an encyclical, says, "Be filled with the Spirit, addressing one another [in] psalms and hymns and spiritual songs, singing and playing to the Lord in your hearts, giving thanks always and for everything in the name of our Lord Jesus Christ to God the Father" (Ephesians 5:18-19).

Now, we should not try to give a technical meaning to the three words "hymn, psalm and song," and suppose that this is already referring to the forms of strophic hymns, biblical psalms, and songs with refrains. What the author is trying to say is this: when you are together, sing all kinds of songs, whether more melodic (*ôdê*) or more rhythmic (*psalmoi*), provided that everything is done in the Holy Spirit. The adjective "spiritual" in fact applies to all three words, even though grammatically it might appear to be linked with only one. It has the meaning of "inspired by the Spirit," as opposed to "free praise." Moreover, we are told to sing with our hearts, that is to say, in a conscious manner, in order to give thanks through Christ to the Father.

Our program of action should always include songs in varied forms, sung with an enlightened faith, carried forth from us by the ineffable groanings of the Spirit, in the name of Christ, for the glory of the Father. But how does this work out in practice?

WHAT IS SUITABLE AND WHAT IS UNSUITABLE

Singing all kinds of music does not mean singing whatever you like, nor does it mean singing in any manner you like. The golden rule is to sing what is appropriate and in a manner that is appropriate for the good of the whole assembly and the quality of the celebration.

Most of the time, this music will not be "the great works," since it needs to be sung by everyone. But simple music is not the same as poor music, and accessible music is not the same as banal music.

All judgment concerning suitability needs to be set in the context of the people who are celebrating together, not starting from aesthetic and cultural criteria imposed by people who are speaking from outside the liturgical action. In order to receive a true impression, you have to be inside, as an active participant of the rites and open to the dimension of faith within the church.

The criterion is therefore this: is it good for praying with? And can you say, "That's beautiful!" in describing the piece? Why was it beautiful? It was beautiful because the assembly was able to make it their own and found it gratifying. The fact that one member of the assembly, following his or her own aesthetic canons, might declare, "That isn't music," does not invalidate the judgment of an assembly which has found such a celebration to be beautiful.

ALL KINDS OF CHANTS

Reading the list "hymns, psalms, and songs," we can see that the celebration requires different modes of vocal expression, depending on the moment in the rite and on what action is taking place.

First of all, there are the acclamations of the whole assembly when the people respond to the greeting of the presiding minister or, through an *Amen*, associate themselves with a prayer made in their name, or welcome the Book of the Gospel, or unite themselves to the chants of the cherubim, "Holy, holy, holy," and so on. These cries, which are stylized in their verbal and vocal forms, make up the spinal cord of the collective ritual action. To leave them out is to deprive oneself of the very basis of singing in unanimity.

In a related genre, there are the litanies whose value is that of an incantation, achieved through the repetition of invocations and the punctuation in time of a succession of petitions. Three moments in the Mass are punctuated by these litanies: the *Kyrie eleison*, the general intercessions, and at the breaking of the bread.

A completely different genre is the recitation of the psalm, where we chew on the word in a pendulum motion that touches the entire body. Two or three notes can suffice, relieved by the singing of the refrain. This is a time when the words of God become flesh within the bodies of men and women.

There are processional chants, lyrical moments that become great through their melodic expansion and quite possibly their harmonic expansion, too. To ritual movements from one point to another (entrance, procession of the book, presentation of the gifts), they add an extra dimension to the purely spatial one, and these chants also receive a special kind of solemnity from the movement that accompanies them.

There are hymns where the act of singing is itself the rite being celebrated and finds its own place, at the Glory to God or in a thanksgiving hymn after Communion.

We need to point out, though, that many assemblies content themselves with the use of just one or two all-purpose genres, such as the song with refrain or the four-part hymn. These songs can be good in themselves, but too often they do not actually take on the thrust of the rite into which they should be inserted. They are always at risk of pushing their own agenda, the mutual exhortation of the group, or a form of piety that is complacent in its devotion through the use of a particular form of sacred music. These songs do have their own value, but they are often better used in groups interested in them than in the ritual act of a church assembly.[20]

CHANTS FOR EVERYONE...
CHANTS BELONGING TO EVERYONE

The infinite variety of types of song that Christian churches have brought to birth in every age and every land should remind us that the celebration is not accessible to all who come to the household of the faith unless there is a sufficient proportion of songs known by and accessible to them.

For centuries, Latin chants ensured the necessary coherence between the people and their repertoire. The last half-century has completely overturned that

---

[20] See the final section of chapter 3 above, p. 28. — Translator

tradition. A media culture has introduced new canons into popular singing at the very moment when the liturgy was seeing the light of day. This has resulted, at least in France, in a huge overproduction of religious songs of all kinds during the past decades.

The hour has come when we need to ask serious questions about this proliferation. If we want to celebrate together, we need to find agreement on a common foundation of ritual songs to be a basis for the liturgical action. Such a choice cannot be made according to the tastes of the day, or as a result of pressure from the media, or by a simple decision by the powers-that-be. We need to gather the consensus of opinions that have already been formed.

Doubtless we will also need to give more attention to traditional songs that are still alive or which are capable of being brought back to life: old Christmas carols, local ethnic chants (e.g., in Brittany), Huguenot psalms, Gallican sequences, pilgrimage hymns, and so on. These melodies were born in the mouths of a people talking the same language, with rhythms that spring naturally from the rhythm of the words, and with a global *ethos* that suits our cultural and Christian gut feelings.

COHESIVE POWER OR CENTRIFUGAL FORCE?

It is important to notice that collective singing and instrumental music, which are among the strongest perceivable signs of cohesion and unity, also carry with them the ongoing risk of focusing attention and sensitivity on themselves, what the great liturgical historian J. A. Jungmann called the centrifugal force of music in the liturgy. The celebration will then become a pretext for the performance of a great work or, less harmfully, an occasion for gratification through singing and playing music that we like.

We can also usefully take note that Western sacred music, from the time of Gallican Gregorian chant onward, was built up almost exclusively from art music (in our particular case, the kind of music cultivated by the church cantors; and later on, the kind of music developed by instrumentalists). Until the Protestant Reformation and the Catholic Counter-reformation, we know almost nothing about popular religious singing. The history of German church music includes the Lutheran chorale in its inheritance, but in the majority of historical studies of French music, popular singing has not been taken into account. Thus a top-ranked German organist will be proud to accompany a congregational chorale. In France, you would run the risk of humiliating such an organist if you asked him to accompany a congregational song. Happily, things are changing.

We need, and in fact we must preserve in the liturgy, all that is beautiful and which leads to the adoration of the one and only God, the *soli Deo gloria* that we find on J.S. Bach's manuscripts. There will be no risk of deviation as long as we are able to say, "I am happy to sing these prayers of the church. I love these songs and I am nourished by them, for they lift me up toward the One whom I celebrate with my brothers and sisters gathered together."

MUSIC AND GRACE

So, music can offer us something quite irreplaceable. Even before the words reach me, the sound of a bell, the strains of an organ, the harmonies of an entrance song, all will touch me in my very depths and, if my spirit is willing, will turn the whole of my being toward the mystery that will be presented.

And when inspired words are resounding, music will be wedded to them, will support them, reinforce them and deepen them. And, in that way, music will play its most specific liturgical role, through all the different genres of music that the liturgy employs.

When finally words are silenced in the presence of that which cannot be expressed, only music will be able to go on beyond, in wonder, in jubilation, in ecstasy.

It would be insane to clip the wings of divine music in the service of God. Such music will always be worthy of something better than either being condemned to silence or being held up as an idol.

The value of sung prayer in common has less to do with the musical notes than with the desire of each person to irrigate both breath and voice, both body and soul, so that the Spirit may seize upon them and make them a river that will flow into the very being of God.

CHAPTER 10

THE EUCHARISTIC PRAYER

"Everything indeed is for you, so that the grace bestowed in abundance on more and more people may cause the thanksgiving to overflow for the glory of God."

2 Corinthians 4:15

At the summit of Christian worship is to be found the Lord's Supper, whose celebration culminates in the eucharistic prayer before being fulfilled in the sharing of the bread.

With good reason it has been said that the most important act of Vatican II's liturgical reform was to give back to the liturgical assembly the possibility of hearing the word of God. But the most daring act of this reform was certainly allowing the same people to hear that great prayer of thanksgiving offered to God for the wonder of the Paschal Mystery. This highest proclamation of the faith of the church had in fact been said by the priest in a low voice and in Latin for more than a thousand years.

While we had already had some experience of the proclamation of the word of God in living languages, we had no such experience of the eucharistic prayer celebrated as an action of the whole assembly presided over by the priest, as described in the General Instruction of the Roman Missal of Paul VI. We only knew written texts; the Roman Canon or ancient Eastern anaphoras. In the West, we had no extant model of this prayer being prayed aloud during the celebration.

At the beginning of the reform, the priest proclaimed the whole text of the prayer aloud in Latin. It quickly became clear that this was unfruitful and even painful. While the rest of the liturgy was being done in the vernacular, why was there this exception at the highest point of the Mass? So the pope authorized modern language translations of the Roman Canon. But then it became clear that this long and difficult text, recited in identically the same way at every Mass, was still of little benefit and was becoming burdensome. So other prayers were prepared, starting both from ancient texts and from contemporary attempts at new texts. Permission was given for the assembly to sing an anamnesis acclamation, a recollection of the paschal mystery after the institution narrative.

Thirty plus years later, what has been achieved?

FROM AN AUDIO-VISUAL POINT OF VIEW

A few years ago, a meeting of those from across Europe who were responsible for televised Masses took place in Paris. The project was to study how the eucharistic prayer unfolded on camera. Fourteen video examples in different languages were viewed. The result was devastatingly sad and boring.

Finally a German-speaking representative stood up and said, "How can we signify that the eucharistic prayer is the praise of the whole assembly addressed to God when a single man at the altar, his eyes riveted to the book, reads a succession of invariable, written words that the people listen to with varying degrees of attention?"

A video from Hungary had still not been played. The representative from this country apologized that there were no televised Masses in his country; but he had brought with him a documentary made in a little town where the liturgy was celebrated according to the Greek Catholic Rite in the Hungarian language. We then watched it.

At the moment of the Great Entrance (the offertory procession), seven men advanced to the iconostasis and intoned the *Cherubikon* in the middle of a crowd standing around them which resembled a moving tide, all singing by heart, while the deacon incensed them, turning all around. Then the priest chanted the Institution Narrative behind the doors, to which all responded with their *Amin*.

It was like a breath of fresh air. If you didn't understand the words, you were still caught up in the festive action of a whole people gathered together. We asked ourselves, "Why, in all the other examples, only words, and in the last example, only mystic festivity? Why not have both at the same time?"

THE CHALLENGE OF THE VOID

We cannot simply resign ourselves to the fact that in our Masses the eucharistic prayer appears to many people who admit with regret that it is the part that is the most empty and the most dead. It is experienced as a long monologue by the priest at the altar, interrupted twice by the singing of the *Sanctus* and the memorial acclamation.

This void in participation by the assembly is felt by many of those responsible for celebrations, and so different practices have arisen to try to remedy the situation. In Eucharists at congresses or ordinations, people have tried adoration responses, sung quietly by the assembly, tied in with the chanting of the two parts of the institution narrative, body of Christ, given for us…. blood of Christ, poured out for us, which corresponds to the two great amens of the Eastern liturgies. People have also tried emphasizing the two moments when the Holy Spirit is invoked, the *epiclesis*, one before the institution narrative (a consecratory epiclesis: Come, Most Holy Spirit of God, make holy for us this bread and this cup); the other after the institution narrative (a communion epiclesis: Fill us, Lord, with your Spirit, that we may become the body of your Christ). Others have also looked for different ways of amplifying the final amen of the prayer in order that this solemn ratification might correspond to the grandeur of what has gone before it.

Open pathways

Are these the right pathways? My testimony is based on a Sunday-by-Sunday practice for over fifteen years in the five parishes for which I was responsible. There we used a form of the eucharistic prayer with nine contributions by the assembly which brought out the underlying rhythm of the prayer: praise-thanksgiving, petitions, doxology, in such a way that the prayer appeared to everybody as the summit of the celebration, alert, intense, unanimous.

But in order to move beneficially and safely in this direction, we need to relearn a number of practices that are essential to oral communication. These practices disappeared centuries ago in our Latin liturgy because of the obligation to read from a book, using a dead language, with the absence of any participation of the assembly, apart, that is, from a look of adoration at the moments of elevation.*

Let us then consider two of the techniques that are essential to oral communication.

---

* Or, as many were taught, the lowering of the gaze, and so *not* looking at this moment. — Editor

"EKPHONESIS"

The Greek word *ekphonesis* means *voice outside,* but it also has a precise technical meaning and is still used in Eastern liturgies. When it is time to pass from the spoken voice to singing, in order that the whole assembly might respond, the celebrant, or the deacon, or a cantor, raises the volume of the pitch. The old Latin Mass also had *ekphoneses* like this. For example, when the priest had read, *sotto voce,* the secret (now called prayer over the gifts) or the end of the Canon and now had to lead into the singing of the preface or the doxology, he chanted, "*Per omnia saecula saeculorum,*" and the cantors responded, "Amen."

This is how the parts for the assembly, at the Sanctus, at the two epicleses, at the adorations after the consecration, at the final doxology, can link in without a break, without anyone having to give the pitch, to the logic of the discourse and the action. This is what we already do with a sung, "Let us proclaim the mystery of faith," to introduce the singing of the memorial acclamation. If the priest does not sing, a cantor can do the *ekphoneses.*

FIXED WORDS AND FLEXIBLE WORDS

No storyteller ever reads from a storybook what he or she is speaking to an audience or recites the text *ne varietur.* If they did, no one would listen. The story being told remains the same; the order of the episodes does not change, nor the keywords that introduce them, like the traditional beginnings of biblical narratives, nor certain other sacred expressions that have become untouchable. But the conjunctive tissue, a certain more flexible filling-out of the structure, allows one to actualize the story, at lesser or greater length according to the circumstances.

These laws were known and practiced in Jewish forms of prayer; it was forbidden to read the prayer, but reflection was required on the manner of saying the prayer, and the same is true of the early centuries of Christianity. Our Eucharistic Prayer II, drawn from the third-century *Apostolic Tradition,* provides a canvas on which the presiding minister was expected to improvise. The variable prefaces of the Roman Mass witness to similar traditions.

If we study the eucharistic prayers we have today, we can say that certain passages, like the one which follows the *Sanctus,* the introduction to the Lord's words in the institution narrative, the intercessions for the church, and those for the living and the dead, are all variable in their formulation even as the overall structure remains in place, as do the keywords which bind the elements together. It is in this profoundly traditional spirit that the eucharistic prayer of the church can be lived out as something *present* on a particular day in a particular assembly.

A PRAYER FOR A MEAL

The eucharistic prayer is not a text that could exist in an isolated state or be said just for itself. It takes on its meaning only when linked to the meal gestures that precede and follow it: the presentation of the gifts and the sharing of bread.

The starting point is the bread and wine that have just been brought up solemnly, accompanied by the singing of an appropriate processional song, gifts which the priest received in his hands and placed on the altar, which has been covered with its altar cloth. And it is from this preparation that will arise what our Greek brothers and sisters call the *anaphora*, that which is carried on high, through the ministry of the one who presides, surrounded by all those invited to the wedding feast of the Lamb.

And when this anaphora is completed, the bread consecrated by that anaphora will be taken in order to be shared out among all.

The mystical meaning of these actions will be fully realized only when they are properly linked together. The Missal of Paul VI did not perfectly articulate the transitions from the presentation of the gifts to the preface and from the doxology to the fraction rite. But since these are only secondary ritual elements, there is nothing to prevent us from using logic to end the procession of gifts and its processional song with the prayer over the gifts that would then move immediately into the preface. In the same way, the Our Father would be followed immediately by the fraction rite. The kiss of peace often intervenes here, breaking the process of interiorization that moves toward Communion. It could easily be repositioned before the offertory.

IN A SINGLE FLOWING MOVEMENT

The dynamic of the eucharistic prayer is something that takes hold of you. If we allow ourselves to be carried away by it, it will draw us into the passage of the Son to the Father in the Spirit.

This eucharistic action is neither linear nor repetitive. It unfolds, as it were, in three waves of praise, thanksgiving and petition, probably following the model of the three Jewish prayers used at festival meals.

The action takes off via three wingbeats thanks to the dialogue which precedes the preface, lifting all of us up together to the place where praise springs forth in wonder at all that God has done and all that God is. This praise, proclaimed before everyone and in the name of everyone (hence the name, *prae-fatio*: that which is said before or in the presence of), soon unfurls into adoration of the Lord of the universe when the whole assembly, uniting itself to the cherubim that Isaiah heard, shouts forth from one to the other: Holy! Holy! Holy! with the song then moving to an invocation that God should save from on high (*Hosanna in excelsis*).

The presiding minister then continues with, "Lord, you are holy indeed," orientating the prayer to thanksgiving for the liberation that God has offered his people. The act of thanksgiving culminates, at the center of the prayer, with the actualizing memory of the paschal mystery of Christ when his death and resurrection are proclaimed. Since this Mystery can only be accomplished by the power of the Holy Spirit, the Spirit's power has been asked for just before the institution narrative, "On the night before he died…." And every time we do once again what he did, his *Pasch* is fulfilled for us, until the day he returns to complete his work.

Now, precisely in the third wave, we need to offer petitions that the coming of the kingdom may be realized, here and now; petitions for those taking part in the celebration, for the whole church, for the world, for the living and the dead, until the time when everything will be recapitulated in the new heavens and the new earth that we await, in the glory of the Father, through the Son, in the Spirit. Amen!

The more the eucharistic prayer is the action of the
assembled church,
the better will be accomplished what the prayer proclaims.

CHAPTER 11

THE WEDDING FEAST OF THE LAMB

"I also saw the holy city, a new Jerusalem,
coming down out of heaven from God,
prepared as a bride for her husband."

Revelation 21:2

HOLY ASSEMBLIES

Paul addressed himself "to the church of God that is in Corinth, to you who have been sanctified in Christ Jesus, called to be holy, with all those everywhere who call upon the name of our Lord Jesus Christ" (1 Corinthians 1:2).

The assembly of the church that is at Corinth is called holy because its members were sanctified by the sending of the only holy one, Christ Jesus, and by the Holy Spirit. Nevertheless, in this same letter Paul strongly reproaches the Corinthians on account of a case of incest, different disputes among the saints themselves, apparent compromises with pagan forms of worship, and above all the way in which they celebrate the Lord's Supper so that "one goes hungry while another gets drunk"(1 Corinthians 11:21).

SINNING MEMBERS

Such is also the state of all our assemblies; they are made holy by Christ's sacrifice, but their members are nevertheless still sinners in their daily lives. Despite being called to a holiness, which is the very holiness of God, and despite having been set free by the Holy Spirit from slavery to evil, they must always work at self-conversion in their struggle against sin.

Now, all our celebrations manifest, or else hide, this tension between a liberation that has already been obtained and the coming of the kingdom that has not yet been achieved. All our rites bear witness to the power of the Holy Spirit at work in the assembly of believers. But this happens of necessity through our anticipation of the new creation that is still undergoing a lengthy and painful process of childbirth.

ALREADY...NOT YET

The credibility of our liturgies derives from the balance maintained between the "already" of the kingdom that has been proclaimed and the "not yet" of the heavenly Jerusalem.

On the one hand, we cannot behave as if we were already in the *parousia*, in the total manifestation and definitive realization of God's plan: "How beautiful it was! I felt as if I were already in heaven!" For in a short while someone will be saying, "Go! The assembly is ended. Return to your homes." At that point, there is a risk of falling down to earth with a bump. Then, at the following assembly, one might perhaps be tempted to hold oneself in reserve, a little cautiously, so as not to be carried away by a dream.

SOBER INSOBRIETY

It is advisable not to run the risk of being reproached for alienating people, not just the foreign observer but also the brother or sister who is less well integrated or has been poorly initiated. But this can happen in certain forms of worship, especially in elements that are perceived as extravagant or expressions of ecstatic fervor that give the appearance of fanaticism.

Drunkenness in the true Spirit is still sober, and ecstasy in the same Spirit is still modest. The gifts of the Spirit are always for the common good and not for the prestige of an inspired member of the gathering. True fervor is to be found in the burning of desire and the intensity of love.

A UNIQUE MOMENT

But on the other hand, what could be sadder and more discouraging than those liturgies, impeccable but frigid, where all the rites are accomplished according to the rules and all the words spoken in their proper place, but without any resonance with the faith which gives meaning and life to these rites being at all perceptible? Nothing kills the rite as much as routine or pure ceremonialism.

How we can produce the perception that what is happening here and now is unique, a freely given and totally new experience that is the promise of the renewal of all things carried out for all believers? How can we give to objects and actions that additional meaning that opens up a limitless pathway toward the new heavens and the new earth?

In the same way as the violinist, with a stroke of the bow, transforms the squealing of a string into a sublime sound capable of captivating and holding in suspense an entire audience in this *becoming-place* where anything can happen, so it is with ministers in worship who, with a stroke of the bow that is their body and under the fingers of the Spirit, open up the words that they utter to unheard-of meanings and transfigure everything that they touch into icons of the invisible.

WAITING FOR THE BRIDEGROOM

But all this will only happen if, in the celebrating assembly, we await the unveiling, the apocalypse of the mystery of the victorious lamb and his bride, the heavenly Jerusalem, who descends from the heavens like a bride adorned for her husband (see Revelation 21:2-9).

How can we wait for the coming of the kingdom here and now, in this little gathering of believers, in a remote corner of the planet, if there isn't the intense desire that it should come? And how can we orient our desire if not by fixing the eyes of our heart and spirit on the accomplishing of all things: the wedding feast of the Lamb?

"Blessed are those who have been called to the wedding feast of the Lamb" (Revelation 19:9). For it is now, in a covenant renewed by a word given and given back, in a meal of bread shared, which is a body given up, that the mystery of the wedding feast enlightens the spirit, warms the heart, and changes the depths of our being by uniting us to our creator and Lord.

MARANATHA

Surely the glorious cross is still at the center of the feast. It is there, before our eyes, while we gather about it. It is the instrument and signifies the mystery of the passage from death to life, the mystery that is fulfilled in the celebration.

But it is not sufficient to recall the passion-resurrection by proclaiming it to be present and active. We still need to anticipate it even while we await the time when it will be achieved: "For as often as you eat this bread and drink the cup, you proclaim the death of the Lord until he comes" (1 Corinthians 11:26).

The most ancient eucharistic prayer, which has come down to us from the earliest days of the church via the book of the *Didache*, ends in the same call that closes the Book of Revelation: "*Maranatha*! Come, Lord Jesus!" There we find the distinctive sign and the scope of the prayer of the assembled Christians.

UNTIL HE COMES!

But it is impossible for us to celebrate this mystery of the end of all things in the now of our liturgies if we have no images of this fulfillment. In this context the most resplendent image seems to be the figure of the wedding feast of Christ and the church.

LIKE A BRIDE DESCENDING FROM HEAVEN

In the book of the Song of Songs, the beloved senses the coming of the beloved whom she awaits. She glimpses him, descending the mountain in mighty leaps. He approaches. He is there. He speaks: "Arise, my beloved, my beautiful one, and go!" (Song of Songs 2:10).*

"Go!" Exactly the same word that the one-and-the-same God said to Abraham: "Go!" Immediately the beloved disappears. She seeks him day and night. She questions everyone she meets, "Have you seen him?" Suddenly, he is there. Then he leaves again. But from now on she knows, "I belong to my lover and for me he yearns" (Song of Songs 7:11). Then in her turn, she can say to him, "Go, my Beloved!" For love is as strong as death. Nothing can extinguish the fire of God any more.

The liturgy plays exactly the same game as the Song of Songs. The voice of God says to us, "Go! I will be with you!" But he still seems to be absent. Hours pass in scrutinizing his words, in deciphering his interventions in the history of humankind, in re-uttering with the psalms the cries for help and the cries of confidence that a people raised to their God. Then the signs of the Covenant are put in place. Now we are taken up in the passage from death to life. The bridegroom gives us for food his body given up for us, for drink he gives us the cup of bitterness and exaltation. Then we hear the word, "Go!" So we return to the world from which he had appeared to be absent but where we will find him in every creature, in every human being, so many sacraments of his love.

---

* English Bible translations all use forms of the verb to come rather than to go. Still, Gelineau's analogy holds, for the beloved and Abraham both give up their own path to follow that of another. – Editor

HE TOOK ON OUR FLESH

The marriage feast of the Lamb with the new Jerusalem that is his church is already there. All the back-and-forth journeys of God toward humanity and of humanity toward God are fulfilled in sacraments and mysteries in the liturgy. Now is when God launches his creation that is the work of his Spirit. Now is when God gives to men and women a heart fit for a love that is always given and always received. Now is when God sends Abraham toward a promised land still to be discovered, and calls Moses in order to provide himself with a people of the covenant. Now is when the Father sends his Son to open once and for all the paschal pathway and to destroy forever the power of evil. The Son bequeaths us his testament: feet washed and body given up.

I AM GOING AWAY…I AM COMING

Today he is absent in order to return to his Father. Today he sends us the Spirit from the Father and chooses us as his witnesses. Today he gathers us together as church, as his body. Today he invites us to the wedding feast of the lamb.

At the end of the Book of Revelation, the journeys to and from heaven and earth cease. In the new heavens and the new earth, God is once and for all in the midst of his people. The new Jerusalem descends like a bride adorned for her husband.

A TREASURE IN EARTHEN VESSELS

If such is the liturgy, how can we not enter into each and every celebration both trembling with fear and full of assurance? What we handle, what is offered to us in the rites, is immeasurable.

Is lack of awareness or lack of competence an obstacle to the presence of the Spirit? This is not a pointless question, for it is true that delicate signs are placed in our fragile hands. We can only be dismayed if we see them turn into counter-signs. "Those songs are out of tune!" "That lector does not know how to read!" "This sermon is worthless!" "All those gestures are just perfunctory!" "This ceremony is interminable!" "No one can pray under such an avalanche of empty words!" "I'm bored to death!"

We need to know these reactions and take account of them as far as we can, without forgetting that the same song can be considered both sublime and intolerable and the same sermon remarkable or barren, depending on the view of each participant. For the liturgy where everything is beautiful, prayerful and well done *for everyone* does not exist. All liturgy is feeble, like everything else in this perishable world of ours.

But at the same time we know that no liturgy, even the poorest and most miserable, can miss the mark completely, since the Spirit is always at work if faith is present. In the same way that an organist who has played a wrong note while improvising can make use of that incongruous note in order to modulate and renew his or her inspiration, the inexhaustible improviser that is the Spirit can make use of our follies and our failures so that the newness of that same Spirit may rise up once again.

The banal phrase of a preacher who is short of ideas can be the very one through which one of the hearers has received a great light. A concert or a spectacle, each the work of human hands, can be a blind alley. A liturgy can never be.

THE LYRE AND THE FINGERS OF THE HAND

Let us, then, enter into liturgy, whether as participants or officiants, after having prepared everything to the best of our ability, material things as well as our hearts, so that we may give ourselves up completely to the action of the Spirit. It is we who have decorated the room and lovingly prepared the wedding feast, the bride's gown, the music and the gifts. When the moment for the festivities arrives, the most important thing is not that everything takes place as we had planned but that the bride/church may descend out of heaven.

We have stretched strings across the frame of the lyre, but it is the fingers of the Spirit that play on them. The important thing is what is going on in the heart of each person; conversion or confirmation, remorse or thanksgiving, questioning or enlightenment, and a joy which nothing and no one can take away from us.

How then can we understand and ensure this in our poor little assembly, local and transitory as it is, fragile and imperfect, always inadequate in its rites, its ministers and its servants, always poor and needy in its members? How can we ensure the fulfillment of the coming of the kingdom in a way that is potentially without limit? How can we ensure that we are all transfigured in such a way that our assembly will itself appear to be "coming down out of heaven from God, prepared as a bride for her husband" (Revelation 21:2)?

SHE DESCENDS FROM HEAVEN

Listen carefully: it is not as if we, all of a sudden, will be transported into heaven; but what we already are is now descending here from heaven. We are that bride, ready to welcome her husband without reserve, in a total exchange of gifts and a perfect union of persons.

But if we do not lift our eyes and hearts high enough, "Lift up your hearts! We lift them up to the Lord!" how can we dare to celebrate? How can we dare to go on about the sacred liturgy at such length and with so many fine-sounding words?

If we are, as it were, consumed by the time of waiting for the wedding day, then we will dare to lay out our rites, rich or poor, austere or sumptuous, with folk both uneducated and educated, saints and sinners, with just a few people or in a large crowd. For it matters little whether our liturgy be the perfumed ointment of great price that Mary lavished on the feet of her Master, or the widow's mite, so long as we are truly among those who have been escorted into the marriage hall with these words:

> *"Come, good and faithful servant,*
> *enter into the joy of your Lord!"*

BOOK TWO

RITUAL ROOTS OF THE
SUNG PARTS OF THE MASS

Prelude

REDISCOVERING THE GIFT OF MINISTRY

THE "SUNG PARTS OF THE MASS"

Musicologists who study the repertoire of sung parts of the Latin Mass from the time of Guillaume de Machaut (ca. 1300-1377) down to our own time consider a "sung Mass" to be made up of five pieces: the *Kyrie, Gloria, Credo, Sanctus* and *Agnus Dei*. A *"Missa Brevis"* (short Mass) has no *Credo*.

Before Vatican II choir members and choir directors distinguished between the sung Mass (*Missa cantata*) and the low Mass (*Missa lecta* [read]). This sung Mass consisted of not just the five pieces typical of the sung Mass described above, but also of the five pieces of the proper of the Mass: the introit, gradual, alleluia, offertory and communion antiphon. The sung texts of the ordinary of the Mass did not change, whereas the sung texts of the proper of the Mass changed according to the liturgical calendar.

A sung Mass also implied that different ministers sing. Priests, deacons and sub-deacons would sing dialogues, prayer, readings, diaconal instructions, prefaces, the Lord's Prayer, and so on. This song distinguished the sung Mass from the low Mass.

Obviously the first issue is this: for several centuries the sung parts of the Mass were considered primarily as a musical repertoire, except where ministers chanted using the ritual tones. This included the body of work known as Gregorian chant, later monodies* (such as the Mass of the Angels and Mass settings by Du Mont, etc.), and accompanied or unaccompanied polyphony, particularly for the Ordinary of the Mass.

A second observation: except in religious communities and the rare parish, this repertoire was reserved either to cantors or to a group of musical specialists (the schola, choir school or choir). Since popular religious songs in the vernacu-

---

* Monody: a melody that is sufficient unto itself. It makes musical sense without chords or harmony. – Translator

lar were not considered as liturgical music, they could be used in low Masses, but not in high Masses.

VATICAN II'S PERSPECTIVE

The liturgical reform of Vatican II suppressed the distinction between the low Mass and sung Mass in order to open to the door to "the full, conscious and active participation" of the assembly (*The Constitution on the Sacred Liturgy* 14), whether it be large or small, rich or poor, whether or not a choir was available, and in whatever language was used. "To promote active participation, the people should be encouraged to take part by means of acclamations, responses, psalmody, antiphons, and songs, as well as by actions, gestures and hearing. And at the proper times all should observe a reverent silence" (*The Constitution on the Sacred Liturgy* 30).

OVERCOMING PAST SHIFTS

It is important to grasp the breadth of cultural change that such a reform movement implies. To understand this well, we must remember the three major shifts that have marked the history of worship in the Roman rite.

1. Beginning in the sixth century, the first shock that Western liturgy experienced was the progressive distancing between the assembly, in principle the first subject of the rites, and the ministers responsible for ritual actions that properly belonged to them.

With the elimination of the catechumenate process, the baptism of the masses of newly converted Barbarians, and the widespread practice of baptizing infants, the faithful no longer benefited from the initiation into the meaning of the church's sacramental life that the fourth-century bishops had provided. The people no longer responded to the psalms or other songs. They *assisted* at Mass. From this time on, singers were responsible for ritual music.

The power of the clerics grew in inverse proportion to the passivity of the faithful. The clerics had the knowledge, the expertise and the sacred character that worship demanded. More and more frequently, they celebrated in those parts of the church to which the faithful no longer had access.

2. Secondly, people understood Latin less and less. The words they said or sang were now divorced from their meaning.

3. Consequently, the assembly could no longer participate in the sung parts of the Mass, which were increasingly the affair of singers and musicians.

The eminent liturgical historian Joseph Jungmann can thus point out the negative effects of the "centrifugal force" of music, particularly in the second millennium. Two practices evolved from this; on one hand, the music covered up the rites, for example, the *Sanctus* and *Benedictus* were sung during the eucharistic prayer, which was said quietly. On the other hand, because the performance of the songs depended on the musicians' competence, the assembly was excluded. We unearth the people's song in the music sung during pilgrimages and devotions, and in religious communities. Unfortunately few traces of these pieces have survived, and historians of music have shown little interest in them.

THE IMPETUS OF THE LITURGICAL REFORM

With inspired boldness, the conciliar liturgical reform set out to repair the damage done in earlier centuries by highlighting:

- the assembly as the primary subject of the celebration,

- the Word of God, proclaimed in the vernacular and explained in the homily, and

- song as the privileged form of the assembly's participation in the rites.

Buoyed along by this impetus, composers and lyricists created a great number of songs for the Mass in most contemporary languages. Some were translations of Latin texts for the ordinary of the Mass and others were original texts for chants of the proper of the Mass. Some were strophic; others were responsorial in form.

Generally speaking, these people tried to create works that respected the rites they were designed to accompany, or of which they were a constituent part, in conformity with the directives of the General Instruction of the Roman Missal (GIRM). Composers made every effort to assure that these pieces were accessible to the assemblies that would sing them.

Initially, composers and lyricists focused on the relationship between text and music. The use of the vernacular forced them to rediscover how words and their meaning, on one hand, and melody and harmonies, on the other, were interdependent in liturgical prayer. One could never overshadow the other. Rather, they were to validate each other as they were sung and prayed.

Underlying the text-music partnership was another more radical partnership of ritual-assembly. Ritual is *for* the assembly, but it exists only *because of* the assembly. Thus biblical proclamation and local culture encounter each other in liturgical celebration. This encounter presupposes a long period of inculturation that has scarcely begun. This is the point of view we have adopted in this book.

There is always the temptation, however, to judge a song for the liturgy by its music first. This approach risks blurring other ritual and communal aspects of the piece. This may explain why, since the council, we have generally neglected the broader field of chant and have, instead, emphasized songs.

How can we reinvigorate research and creativity in liturgical song while honoring both tradition and the direction of the liturgical reform?

AVAILABLE SOURCES AND MODELS

Among all the sensory elements of which Christian liturgy is composed, the musical element is the most fluid, the most evolving and the most diversified. Sounds are fleeting.

Before Guido d'Arezzo created hexachordal notation in the 11th century, Western liturgical music was only transmitted orally. Therefore, we cannot be sure that what was passed down to us conserved the melody and rhythm of a piece of music. Above all, and most essential for liturgy, we do not know how it actually had been sung in the context of the sacred action. We have a fairly reliable sense of the notes of the melodies of the Gregorian corpus, but we do not know how the singers sang them. Isidore of Seville, Alcuin, and others certainly left us interesting spiritual and anthropological considerations of the act of sacred song, but we do not know how these were translated vocally. For example, the intervals between the degrees of the modal scales were clearly not tempered.

Once they had scores to decipher, musicologists turned their attention primarily to these written works. But as we have already noted, in the majority of cases this is the specialized music of the cantors. We know almost nothing about the popular music of the Middle Ages, whether sacred or secular.

Things changed with the Reformation. Luther's *Kirchenlieder,* Calvin's *Genevan Psalter,* and the varied hymns of the Anglican tradition present us with popular sacred music. But since Catholic liturgy excluded all but Latin chants, only in the world of non-liturgical religious songs do we find models of sacred congregational song.

This is an extremely precious source for understanding the features of popular French-language religious song. But the forms of the noëls or the different types of popular religious songs represent only a fraction of the kinds of sung words considered to be part of the rites.

And if we wanted to borrow melodies and ways of singing from our current media culture, what criteria would we use to do so?

A FUNDAMENTAL PRINCIPLE

In its chapter on music, the Constitution on the Sacred Liturgy of Vatican II assigns a certain *munus ministeriale* to music as its reason and meaning. These two Latin words are difficult to translate properly. If we say that in a celebration music fulfills a ministerial function, we will get one of several responses: "What does this jargon mean?"; people may then look disappointed and mumble, "That's all?" or protest vehemently, "Any music worthy of the name should be called something better than 'functional.'"

However, everything comes together in these words. In worship that is "service" or "ministry," as the Greek root of the word "liturgy" indicates, everything that is done, said, shown or heard is "rite"; an element of a symbolic whole. Whenever there is song, its root meaning comes first and foremost from the ritual action that is taking place, not from the music.

Those engaged in liturgical ministry who would rediscover the ritual foundations of the different forms of liturgical singing face many challenges. What we say here about music is just as true of gestures and postures, of objects and images, of styles of prayer, as it is of styles of songs.

The liturgical movement that prepared the way for and followed Vatican II began with what was then obvious and valid: the need for people to understand and participate actively. Several decades of working with the reform have heightened our sensitivity to how deeply liturgy is rooted in our bodies, to how richly biblical it is, and to its aesthetic aspects.

However, the role of song has too often been marginalized within liturgical action. Then we risk song as something that keeps us busy without examining the rite in question. More or less interchangeable songs are slotted into the celebration here or there. "What will we sing today? Why? Because we know it and like it!" Undoubtedly this approach has in some ways helped the assembly to pray, but have we really shed light on the specific role of liturgical song? Do we know how to explain its specific grace?

REFLECTING ON THE BIG PICTURE

The purpose of this book is not just to study the musical form of each of the sung parts of the Mass, although delineating each individual part would not be a waste of time. It is more important, however, to understand how the liturgy adopts or generates different sung forms according to its rites, words, gestures, places, ministers and assemblies. Therefore liturgical ministry involves choosing or creating the verbal and musical underpinnings that best reveal the nature of the celebration of the Christian mysteries: praise of God the Father by his incarnate Word in the breath of the Holy Spirit.

To do this, we begin where rite, word and sound meet (Chapter 1). Following that, we will classify the sung parts of the Mass by type and study what characterizes each part.

Chapter 1

THE ACOUSTIC WORLD
OF CHRISTIAN WORSHIP

Christian worship is a social, collective human activity in which the cries of human anguish and joy, the proclamation of the Good News that saves, and the praise of the redeemed resound together. Ear and voice engage the whole human person in this ritual action.

Every religious tradition offers prayers of petition and sings hymns. Some recite sacred texts in a ritual manner. But the proclamation of salvation belongs to the world of biblical revelation.

In Christian worship, the proclamation of the saving Word occupies an essential place. This proclamation changes key according to a rich palette of acoustic and verbal behaviors. The relationship between words and their pitch is constantly being re-established.

Thus Christian liturgies run the whole gamut of our verbal and musical forms of expression to offer those celebrating a rich variety of ways to be before the Mystery.

However, these many forms have only been partially tapped and are unevenly developed. In some celebrations, prescribed texts are recited in the same neutral and uninspired tone. At the other extreme, in some celebrations where one song follows another, words seem only to be a pretext for music.

Studying the different forms of the sung parts of the Mass of the Roman rite can help us better appreciate what a sung liturgy offers in terms of our relationship to God in the Spirit, thanks to the different symbols of the ritual.

The illustration below indicates the rich palette of possible forms of Christian song.

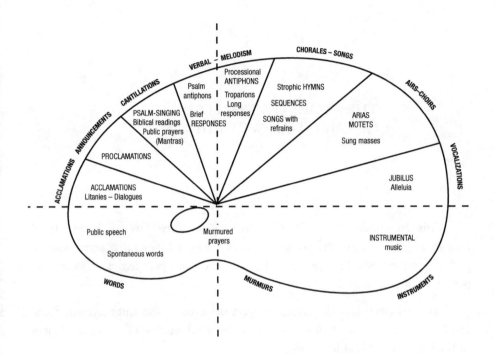

THE THRESHOLD BETWEEN SPEECH AND MUSIC

This palette is made up of two levels of ritual words. At the bottom, are modes of expression that can be called "spoken" in contrast to the "sung" words that characterize the upper portion of the palette.

The threshold is delineated by the appearance of a specific pitch in our speech. The tone in question does not just include what today we call "music": a melody composed of identifiable notes whose frequencies we can determine according to the notes of an existing scale. Before pitch becomes song in the strict sense of the word, it can enter a realm that falls between ordinary speech and song.

At this stage, the tone of voice first implies a special relationship between the speaker; an announcer, a storyteller, a reader, someone giving an order, etc., and their hearers, seen or unseen. It is always determined and perceived by social convention.

This tone becomes music when an air or a melody can be set to notes and reproduced. This is as true today of chant or psalmody as it is of an antiphon or a hymn.

Adding a rhythmic element—reciting a poem, citing a proverb, collective reciting of common prayers—more clearly indicates the presence of music.

THE RELATIONSHIP BETWEEN WORDS AND MUSIC

The sound palette is also designed around a vertical pole that delineates a point of balance between words and music in the horizontal series of song forms. The more we move to the left, the more words dominate; the more we move to the right, the more music takes the upper hand.

Spoken Words

Under the threshold I have indicated three types of spoken words.

Murmurs

From the depths of our being arise murmurs, of anguish or contentment, of play or prayer. An example of this is the recitation of the rosary either alone or with a group. All affective cerebral and muscular activity is concentrated in the mouth where the word is simultaneously produced and consumed. Expressing this prayer both constitutes and interiorizes it. The best ritual example of this is the Our Father of the Mass prayed quietly by all the members of the assembly. In this instance each person can interiorize the words deeply.

Spontaneous speech

When they have "something to say" to the public, representatives of a group use a ritual tone without trying to or being conscious of it. They think they are expressing themselves naturally and spontaneously, but the natural and spontaneous do not exist in a pure state. Those who speak in this way are only interested in everyday oral communication.

Public speech

When someone reads a text, speaks a prayer or makes a declaration before the assembly, they must take on the role associated with that act. Even if that person does not assume an identifiable ritual tone, the register, intensity and delivery of their voice change. If it does not, they will not fulfill their role.

To assure that certain texts, especially those recited collectively (the Glory to God, the Creed, etc.), have the appropriate dignity, they need a certain rhythm and place in the tonal range. Lacking this they cannot signify as they should; they become a-ritual, even unbearable.

Words That Have Musical Sounds

Exclamations

The exclamation is the first manifestation of the power that musical sound brings to a word. Consider a groan, "Arggh!"; an exclamation, "Yippee!"; a wail, "Oh no!"; an ovation, "Bravo!" This power comes from rhythm, melody, and even the way the sound floats. It comes from the investment of breath and voice it demands.

Sometimes the sound is sustained: "Yip-pee-ee!" Sometimes the word is repeated rhythmically: "Bra-vo, bra-vo!" It both signals something and is emotionally charged.

Whether individual or collective, the spontaneous exclamation that we find in some prayer groups, or in freely structured worship services, is exceptional in European Christian liturgy. If integrated into Christian worship, the exclamation is usually given a stylized form. In this case its rhythmic structures and melodic line are such that everyone can be caught up in them. We do not call these exclamations, but identify them using more specific words. Among these are the "Amens," "Alleluias," and "*Maranathas*" that have come into our worship vocabulary without being translated, as well as the Greek expression, *Kyrie eleison*. The French formulas pertain mostly to responses to greetings and the prayers of the faithful.

The liveliness of these ritual exclamations is a touchstone of the authenticity of a liturgical celebration.

Announcements

The role of an announcement is to transmit messages or information in the most understandable and effective way possible. Words, buttressed and accompanied by pitch, play an essential role in this. I call these warnings or reminders "monitions." They are neither occasional nor one-time spoken interventions made during a celebration, but ritually structured word acts.

Our different liturgical traditions have often entrusted announcements to the deacon: "Let us go forth in peace," he invites, as a procession begins; "Go in the peace of Christ" at the end of Mass; "Catechumens, go!" after the Liturgy of the

Word; "Let us offer each other the sign of peace," before sharing in holy communion; "Attention! Silence!" before the eucharistic prayer, and so on.

The deacon's most important intervention is to announce the intentions of the prayers of the faithful in such a way that the whole assembly can pray for what has been stated. The most solemn diaconal proclamation is the *Exsultet* of Holy Saturday.

Today all these functions of announcing have been spread among different ministers.

By the greeting, "The Lord be with you," or its equivalent formulas, the presider announces to the assembled faithful the Lord's presence among his people. The presider proclaims, "The mystery of faith" in the Eucharist, and in all the blessing formulas pronounced over the bread and wine, over water and over the people. The highest form of proclamation is found in the prefaces of the great blessing prayers that describe the mystery being celebrated.

The tone used for these announcements distinguishes them from other ritual word acts. Short announcements often use two or three notes, "The Lord be with you" or "Go in the peace of Christ." More developed announcements, such as the intentions of litanies, use tones that often resemble more closely those of cantillation.

Cantillation

Cantillation constitutes the largest body of ritual chants within the traditions of Christian worship. "Cantillation" is a word coined by some contemporary musicologists to designate the readings or prayers of Jewish and Christian ritual that use a special tonal pattern. In chant, the melody takes the lead. Cantillation, however, uses the length of notes and their pitch to direct the movement of syllables so that listeners understand correctly the meaning of the biblical text that is being read. In general musicology, this would be called recitative. Cantillation refers to a specific way of reading the Bible in the Judeo-Christian tradition.

There are three principal groupings of cantillated texts in the liturgy: biblical readings, public prayers, and psalmody itself.

In every culture, a certain pitch, whether spoken or chanted, characterizes the public reading of important written records. The foremost example of this in the Judeo-Christian tradition is the Bible. "Whoever reads the Word without cantillating it is an idolater," says the Mishna. Depending on the era, the cultural milieu, and the degree of solemnity, people have used tones that are either closer to speech or closer to cantillation.

Because there seems to be an absolute split between speech and song in our modern Western culture, cantillation is perceived as song. But most cultures lay claim to intermediate pitches of public speech that lie between our experiences of "spoken" and "sung." This makes it worthwhile to address cantillation here, not first as song, but as public sacred speech. Recitatives that are over-sung can drown the words in the *mélos* (melody).

Because of the poetic structure of the psalm-poem, psalmody constitutes a very specific type of cantillation in Christian worship. I will deal with it when we speak of the psalm in the Liturgy of the Word at Mass.

Verbo-Melodism

As the two words wedded into the single expression "verbo-melodism" indicate, the type of song designated by this expression involves two equal partners: on one hand the *logos* (the word, a discourse*), and on the other hand the *mélos* (music, singing). Each is at the service of the other; neither dominates.

Contemporary liturgical musicology invented the expression verbo-melodism** to designate that trait considered most characteristic of Christian singing: the most profound symbiosis possible in the interaction of words and *mélos.* In this marriage, the melody can no longer be separated from the words of which it was born. From this melody, each syllable receives its own timbre, length, pitch and intensity.

Here the music appears to expand the words even as they are being uttered. Musical, too, are the dynamism of consonants and the vowel color of syllables in the announcement. Above all, this music offers poetic access to the mystery being celebrated, moving us to petition, contemplation and praise. One with the words of the prayer, the music does not use the syllables of the text for its own ends. We find the most beautiful models of this type of song in the best pieces of the Gregorian repertoire, in the introits, for example.

It can be argued that the majority of ritual songs found in the great Christian liturgical traditions depends either on cantillation or verbo-melodism. This is not surprising in a religion founded on a revelatory word that each celebration is intended to actualize. It is not simply a case of reminding

---

* This comes from the French word *verbe*, used to translate the Greek word *logos*, which English would translate as "word," as in "the Word was made flesh" (*le Verbe s'est fait chair*). – Translator

** The expression "verbo-melodism" is also used in *Music and Liturgy: The Universa Laus Document and Commentary* (Pastoral Press, 1988). – Translator

ourselves of doctrinal content through biblical words or doctrinal formulas. In song and praise this word, celebrated as a sacrament of the covenant between God and humanity, actualizes this covenant within the communion of the church.

Within this immense repertoire, we can distinguish words and melodies as one would distinguish the two partners in a marriage. One, more sober, remains almost syllabic: a note corresponds to each syllable. The other, more lyrical, adorns certain syllables with several expressive notes grouped together as neumes. In these two cases, as we will see, the music is wedded to the notes to reveal their intellectual content and to let us discover their spiritual flavor.

PSALM REFRAINS AND BRIEF RESPONSES

The most syllabic example of verbo-melodism can be found in the refrains sung by the assembly between the verses of the responsorial psalm. For example:

No-tum fe-cit Do-mi-nus, al-le-lu-ia,   Sa-lu-ta-re su-um, al-le-lu-ia.

Once the psalmody was reduced to a few verses, we ended up with brief responses with a shortened refrain between the remaining verses. And, when the refrains between the verses of the psalm disappeared, what had been the refrain became the sung antiphon that frames the beginning and the end of each psalm that typifies the psalms in today's Liturgy of the Hours.

We find two types of these psalm refrains or short antiphons. First, there are the model formulas, whose melody is already known, to which the words of different texts have been adapted. This is the case of the refrain *Notum fecit Dominus* (see above). Dozens of antiphons have been set to it. Second, there are the melodies crafted specially for the text. To help you get a better sense of this, let us look at an example of an antiphon from the office of the dead, using a French text:

Si   tu re-tiens nos pé-chés,   qui donc, Sei-gneur, pour-ra sur-vi-vre ?

ANTIPHONS SUNG IN PROCESSION OR WHILE STATIONARY

With the fifth century came the development of the *troparion* parallel to the development of the psalm refrains whose texts generally came from the Psalter in use. The word *troparion* means a "little air" and plays on two of the meanings of "air"; it "has the air of," and it is "an air," a melody. Because its text is generally very simple, those who are singing it can grasp it readily so they can proclaim, bring to life and meditate on the mystery of the day:

> Today the angel Gabriel comes to Nazareth
> and greets the young woman Mary.

> With him we greet her:
> Rejoice, Mary, blessed among women.

Sometimes the melody is built on an existing fragment by reworking the known tune to match new words. Sometimes it is an original melody that highlights the text, clause by clause and word by word, as we see in the Gregorian introits.

This type of chant, whether it be a *troparion* or grand antiphon, was used as much for processional antiphons (entrance, offertory, etc.) as for stational antiphons to the *Magnificat*, the *Benedictus* or a song to the Virgin. This is also the same type of response used for the office of Matins.

In each of these cases, the antiphon or the "stanza" (as it is called in the new *troparia*[*] created in French since Vatican II) is most often extended by one or several verses sung by soloists. If the stanza concludes with an acclamation or an invocation that serves as a refrain, such as "Rejoice, Mary, blessed among women," as in the example quoted above, everyone sings this refrain between the verses and at the end of the song.

ANCIENT HYMNODY IN LYRICAL PROSE

We can also include with verbo-melodism the song of the most ancient Christian hymns written in lyrical prose before the advent of metrical hymnody at the end of the fourth century. Included here would be the evening hymn, "Joyful Light of Heavenly Glory," the Glory to God incorporated into the Roman Mass, and the *Te Deum*. One or several typical melodic formulas

---

[*]The *troparion* is a new form of liturgical song that appeared for the first time in French in 1966. The term is borrowed from the Byzantine tradition. It is composed of a stanza sung by a small group of singers or a choir, a refrain in which the whole assembly can join, and verses sung by a soloist or choir. Sometimes the whole assembly can join in the stanza. It is designed to introduce us to some aspect of the mystery of Christ.
– Translator

are adapted to successive phrases of the text. We can cite, for example, the *Gloria XV*, written in Mode III, which takes us back to the Mediterranean origins of Christian chant:

Glo-ri-a — in ex-cel-sis De-o   Et in ter-ra pax ho-mi-ni-bus bo-næ vo-lun-ta-tis.

Lau - da - mus te.   Be - ne   -   di - ci - mus te...

Musical plainchant

Under the heading of verbo-melodic chant we can also include the important seventeenth century French creation called musical plainchant, of which the Masses of Du Mont are the most popular and well-known examples. It is astonishing that this model has not inspired similar worthy efforts in French since the reform of Vatican II.

Strophic Hymns and Songs with Refrains

Strophic hymns and songs with refrains bring us to the forms that composers and lyricists since Vatican II have most often used for new liturgical songs in modern languages. The reason for this is clear: these forms lend themselves most readily to the song of the assembly.

The metered hymn

The strophic hymn follows this principle: The text to be sung is written in verses whose rhythmic structure is identical from one verse to the next:

- each verse has the same number of lines;

- each line has the same number of syllables,
  depending on where the line falls in the verse; and

- each line uses the same internal verbal rhythm; the breaks
  and conjunctions between the words that create meaning
  fall in the same place from one verse to the next.

This symmetry between the verses, which is called isorhthym, allows composers to use the same music without change from one verse to the next.

An historical overview indicates the varied fortunes of this style of hymn in the liturgy.

The account in St. Augustine's *Confessions* (IX, 7) attributes the introduction of the metered hymn into the West to St. Ambrose, Bishop of Milan, who was imitating the practice of St. Ephrem of Syria. Augustine recounts this in his description of the events of Holy Week of the year 386 in which he participated with his mother St. Monica.

Ambrose wanted to bolster the courage of his people, who were besieged by the Arian soldiers of the Empress Justina in the Portian Basilica on the outskirts of Milan. To do this, Ambrose wrote four-line verses. Each line was composed of four iambic feet (one short, one long[21]), a very popular Latin meter. No doubt this pastoral bishop used music the people knew. Here is a hypothetical restoration of a melody preserved in Milan using an authentic Ambrosian text:

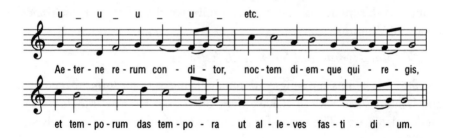

We do not know whether the people sang all the verses or whether—which is, in fact more likely—following the Syrian model of Ephrem, a cantor chanted the verses, and the people responded with a refrain that used the same meter and same melody as the end of the verse.

Ambrose's hymns enjoyed lasting success and a school of hymn-writing sprang up. All during the Latin Middle Ages, poets created thousands of "Ambrosiana," but the original Latin meter was no longer observed. When counting syllables, the Latin accent was more or less taken into account. However, the people no longer sang these hymns, which from this time on became the repertoire of the scholas

---

[21] It is important to note that in the iambic rhythm, the rhythmic emphasis is on the short (whereas, in French, we have the tendency to come off the short and emphasize the long).

or monastic choirs. Still, some medieval hymn melodies did inspire popular songs in the vernacular, both religious and secular.

Thus it was that at the time of the Reformation, Luther and his followers created a popular hymnody for worship. Originally it was inspired by traditional Latin hymns, but later composers created hymns using a variety of sources.

This period was an intense time of hymn creation:

- the German *Kirchenlieder,* called *chorals* in French;

- the 150 psalms of the Genevan Psalter and its imitators; and

- Anglican hymns and their innumerable descendents.

However, in the Roman liturgy it was forbidden to use songs in the vernacular, especially after the Council of Trent (1545-63). In the Catholic world of the Counter-Reformation, popular religious hymnody developed outside the liturgy: in catechism sessions for children and adults; in popular missions, which developed in France especially after the seventeenth century; in devotions, especially Benediction of the Blessed Sacrament; and finally and without interruption from the Middle Ages to our own day, in the inexhaustible tradition of Christmas carols which has given us some pure masterpieces. Sometimes these pieces are structured as strophic hymns and sometimes as songs with refrains.

Noteworthy here is the very remarkable hymn form that we find in various carols, and in many songs that probably originated in Brittany. Many of these are old French melodies that have been preserved because seventeenth century missionaries set Breton texts to these tunes. This is the form AA-BA, or its variants, such as AB-AB, etc. The melodic repetitions facilitate and intensify everyone's participation in the singing without weakening the text, which is not repeated. This cultural form is still valuable today.

As an example of a melody with this internal structure, let us take the fifteenth(?) century carol, *A la venue de Noël* ("When Christmas comes"), which is constructed on the ABAC form:

The openness of the post-Vatican II liturgy to vernacular languages gave rise to an enormous creative movement in the area of traditional strophic hymnody, as well as in the area of songs with refrains. This latter movement was already well developed in French between 1940 and 1950.

The principal appeal of the strophic hymn is its use in the beginning of each "hour" of the Liturgy of the Hours, which calls for a hymn. Here the sung rite is the act of communal song itself. The text is linked with the time of day, the day, or the feast.

The possibility of introducing a hymn after communion gives new appeal to this form, as we will see. Thus we actually have at our disposal several hundred strophic hymns, with their texts and music. They provide important witness to the role of music in contemporary liturgical song.

Songs with refrains

The vernacular song was born of popular devotion, and has no ritual roots in the official Catholic liturgy. In addition, this song form with its refrain is not proper to the liturgy. It is frequently used in popular songs. Nonetheless, it is the form that has been most used in the Mass since vernacular usage was authorized.

From the point of view of the relationship between the text and music, which is our central concern here, the metrical rule—isorhythm—that regulates the lines of the verses of a song is the same as that for the verses of a hymn.

The presence of a refrain that stands on its own offers the assembly the chance to participate more fully, using simple words that work their way deep into our memories and hearts.

The sequence

The sequence is constructed of a free series of paired verses; the tune that was just sung with one text by choir A is immediately taken up by choir B using another text. This continues as necessary, using other melodies for each new pair of verses whose texts can vary in length (e.g. the *Veni Sancte Spiritus* or the *Dies Irae*). The music clearly takes the lead, even if the text develops according to its own logic.

In contrast to the hymn form, the sequence form interests us because it introduces a new melody after two similar verses. This preserves complete liberty as to the length and rhythmic structure of each pair of verses.

Of the some five thousand known sequences that were created in the Middle Ages, the post-Tridentine liturgy retains only four. While this form has not been tapped in recent creations of liturgical song, it would be of great interest, as we shall see, for the meditation hymn.

Hymns and songs provide an inexhaustible gold mine of song for the assembly's participation in liturgical celebrations. But their lushness and their accessibility should not eclipse the other forms of ritual song that the liturgy demands.

Motets, Masses and Cantatas

A repertoire that can properly be called "musical" began developing around the middle of the Middle Ages in churches that were well endowed with musical resources such as cantors, choir directors, soloists, organs and instruments. Music history has directed its interest almost exclusively toward this repertoire: motets, Masses, responses, lamentations, *Dies irae*, *Te Deum*, vespers, *Magnificat*, and so on.

Even if composers were bound by the texts they used, even if they were more or less inspired by the content of the sung words, and even if they were conscious that they were doing something religious, we are here dealing with what is currently called "sacred music." Music takes the lead; music can be sufficient all by itself. For this reason, music can move from the liturgy to the concert stage where it is valued as repertoire, detached from the rites from which it was born.

It is fair to observe that, since the beginning, the great musical works have been connected only with a small number of worship spaces, primarily cathedral churches and the courts of princes. By the nineteenth century, when more parishes were sufficiently well-off to support choirs and acquire organs, two poles seemed to have emerged: the ritual pole, the sanctuary; and the musical pole, the choir loft. Sandwiched between them were the people who assisted at Mass and listened to the music.

We should not be astonished that the recent rediscovery of participation of the people in the rites by word, postures and especially song, illustrates the religious and cultural gap between the earlier practices to which we have referred and today's. It is easy to understand why the treasures of sacred music are often more at home in spiritual concerts than in the celebration of the Eucharist.

This gap between the works of the past and today's assemblies does not directly affect the use of soloists, polyphony or musical instruments in the liturgy. Everything depends on how these elements are integrated into the ritual action and into the assembly's life and repertoire.

Polyphony

What can be said of polyphony can also be said of soloists, the organ and other instruments. Their contribution is good if it serves the rite and the assembly. Their contribution becomes questionable when the voice or the instrument distracts from the celebration and focuses the celebration on the performer.

With this in mind, we can argue that polyphony can accompany in a positive way almost all the types of singing that we have examined, but its effect will vary in each instance.

1. IN ACCLAMATIONS. Enhancing the assembly's "Amen" or "Thanks be to God" by the richness and brilliance of harmony bolsters the sense of a common acclamatory gesture.

2. IN PSALMODY. Superimposing the recitation of the verses of a psalm over several voices is often called a *faux-bourdon*. If the solemn chanting in harmony of the *Magnificat* or some isolated verses in a *troparion* or a processional alternates with the assembly's unison, polyphony is a festive addition. But ordinarily polyphony risks choking the communal recitation of a psalm and drowning words in a mass of sound. Punctuation that marks out meaning is blurred or disappears. Syllables are mechanically equalized. There is a risk that the Word of God will be the loser.

3. IN VERBO-MELODISM. Monody is presumed when the *mélos* is wedded to the words. But in a *troparion,* polyphony can be used in a refrain if it does not compromise the unison, in verses sung by two or three soloists, and even in the refrain if the harmonization makes its message clearer.

4. IN HYMNS, CHORALES, AND SONGS. The musical style of the melody dictates whether polyphony is appropriate, as it would be in a classical chorale, for example, or inappropriate because it would change the nature of a simple monody.

These remarks about polyphony do not apply to hummed accompaniments.

Faced with the treasury of sacred music, the fruit of Western culture and witness to its faith, we must discern carefully whether we can re-use it in today's liturgy. We must not ostracize it and we must avoid aestheticism. In each case we must judge what is good for *this* assembly in *this* situation.

Vocalizations

In the promptings of desire, in the offerings of gratitude, in pleading or in thanksgiving, words fail at some point. They suffice neither for what the soul wants to say nor for what the Spirit murmurs to our own spirit in her ineffable language. At this point, the unadorned voice or pure music can express the passion of the heart.

The liturgy has not excluded this wordlessness from its song. We hear it in the plaintive cry that haunts the pronunciation of each letter of the Hebrew alphabet (*aleph, beth,* etc.) at the beginning of the verses in the Lamentations. We find it above all in the *jubilus* that often embellishes the last syllable of the word "alleluia." Other songs or prayers[22] can lead us to that outpouring of our soul that St. Augustine spoke of so well:

> He who sings a *iubilus* does not pronounce any words; he utters a wordless sound of joy; it is the voice of his soul pouring forth happiness as intensely as possible, expressing what he feels without adverting to any particular meaning. To manifest his joy, the man does not use words that can be pronounced or understood, but he just allows his happiness to burst forth without any words; his voice then seems to express a joy so intense that he is incapable of formulating it.[23]

Instrumental Music

Beyond words are instruments. When an inspired instrumentalist plays a solo, he or she can offer the assembly a marvelous entry into prayer. An instrumental ensemble is not excluded, but inserting it in the ritual action is often a more delicate proposition.

> Though man may find in his own voice the musical instrument which is closest to his heart, for it ever accompanies him in all his joys and sorrows, he nevertheless has other means, more powerful and subtle, for expressing himself in that world of sound which his own spirit has created. In nature, secretly in tune with himself, he found reeds more docile to his breath, strings more supple under his fingers and shells more sensitive to his impacts. He has made such things even more human than himself, capable of weeping or laughing, of understanding or of loving, even of praying and adoring. It is not merely his own flesh

---

[22] Here we can consider the gift of speaking in tongues of which certain forms, collective or individual, are related to singing without words. These practices are found more often in prayer groups than in the eucharistic liturgy.

[23] *Enar. in Ps.* 99, 4 (*PL* 37, 1272). Cited in Joseph Gelineau, SJ, *Voices and Instruments in Christian Worship,* translated by Clifford Howell, SJ (Collegeville, The Liturgical Press, 1964), 26.

which groans in travail waiting for the sons of God to be made known, but the whole of creation with him; it is not only the redeemed, who are to give thanks to God, but with them the whole universe, first fruits of the new heavens and the new earth.[24]

And beyond sound is that to which all music must lead us: the silence that speaks the ineffable.

---

[24] Joseph Gelineau, SJ, *Voices and Instruments in Christian Worship*, translated by Clifford Howell, SJ, (Collegeville, The Liturgical Press, 1964), 26-27.

CHAPTER 2

PROCESSIONALS

The liturgy is structured to a certain degree by five processions and their songs: the entrance of the cross, the entrance of the Book, the procession with the gospel book, the procession with the gifts, and the communion procession. By studying the rites that belong with each song, we will see which musical forms best suit each part of the celebration.

THE ENTRANCE SONG

The first rite of the Mass includes a processional song: "After the people have assembled, the entrance song begins as the priest and the ministers come in" (GIRM 25).

The Four Ritual Functions

Number 25 of the GIRM assigns four ritual functions to the entrance song:

1. to "open the celebration,"

2. to "intensify the unity of the gathered people,"

3. to "lead their thoughts to the mystery of the season or feast," and

4. to "accompany the procession of priest and ministers."

Let us examine these four aspects of the rite more closely.

1. The entrance song begins both the Mass and the opening rites, the unit of transitional rites that extends from the opening song to the opening prayer inclusive. This first song draws us actively into the celebration.

2. Before the entrance hymn, all have found their place. Up until this point, everyone has acted individually, including those who have greeted their neighbors and those participants who have not yet entered. By giving all a part in this first ritual action, the entrance song ritually constitutes the assembly as assembly. Common song is a privileged means of signifying this unity in an appropriate manner. Bodies will always remain side by side, only voices can be fused as one in a perceptible manner. Even if all do not sing, the assembly praises God as the assembly.

3. Song unites voices both by rhythm and melody as well as by words that speak the day's mystery or one of its aspects. Thus the text provides a focus for the spirits of those who enter into celebration.

4. The primary purpose of this first sung part of the Mass is to accompany the entrance of the presider and his ministers. This is why it is by nature a processional. In certain instances, the whole assembly or part of it (catechumens, first communicants, spouses, etc.) may enter behind the cross. But ordinarily, only the ministers enter. We recognize that in the liturgical assembly, all do what one does as the servant of all. Such is the power of the procession down the center aisle; it is as though it draws the whole assembly into the movement toward the rising sun, the risen Christ.[25]

Entrance and/or Opening?

The word "entrance" used here is ambiguous because it can be interpreted in two ways: either as the physical entrance of participants into the body of the church, or as the beginning of the celebration. "Entrance song" implies both.

---

[25] Some additional reflections on the link between ritual and song for the entrance:

- Please, let the figure of Christ on the processional cross be not that of a dead man but that of the risen Christ who intercedes for us with the Father.
- If there are too many visual symbols in the entrance procession, they end up canceling each other out. For instance, it could be meaningful to reserve the entry of the Lectionary for the Liturgy of the Word (see below, the procession with the book).
- It is not always opportune for the presider to be in the procession. With the rest of the assembly, he can be singing to welcome the cross before bowing before it. This emphasizes adoration and the sign of the cross.
- Finishing the song at the same time as the procession, when the cross is placed in its stand, gives a strong signal. The silence then draws attention to what follows.
- The sign of the cross is more powerful if the celebrant—and eventually, the whole assembly—chants it (see *MNA* 37. 11 bis).

There is a certain ambiguity in the GIRM. It indicates that opening the celebration is the first function of the entrance song, yet the procession of the ministers that the song accompanies is the first rite of the celebration.

This ambiguity is in part responsible for the fact that many people keep the song as the opening, but neglect the procession.

The Procession

The GIRM (82) indicates that the entrance procession constitutes the opening of the Mass with a congregation. The ritual movement not only allows all the participants to "enter with" the procession in spirit, but it also conditions the type of song that should be used and its processional nature.

Carrying candles, incense, the lectionary and the cross in front of the procession is optional. Each element acts on the assembly in its own symbolic fashion, provided that the signs are perceptible and well adapted. However, in this case, the most important symbol is the processional cross: the Lord comes among his people, inviting them to follow him. The cross, sign of his paschal victory, is placed before the altar, facing the whole assembly. The cross makes sense of, orients and gives meaning to the procession and the assembly of the baptized.

After the silence that follows the end of the song, it would be good for the presider, who is standing before the cross, to bow profoundly and solemnly intone "In the name of the Father…" as he slowly makes the sign of the cross. Thus the members of the assembly would also feel invited to adoration as they bow and make the sign of the cross in memory of their baptism.

A Processional Song

According to the ritual, the entrance song is not sung for its own sake. It accompanies a primary sign, the movement of persons in space and time. Among the forms of song that are used at the beginning of the Mass, all are not equally processional in nature.

Three forms lend themselves best to the procession:

1. Litany. The most processional of the song forms is the litany in which brief prayers sung by one or two cantors alternate with an invocation by the people. The traditional model of this invocation is the *Kyrie eleison*.

    The typical example is found in the Litany of the Saints that used to be sung during the processions for the feast of St. Mark and for rogation days.[26]

---

[26] See pages 141-142 for the six alternating forms that the litanies of the saints contain.

A shortened version used at the Easter vigil makes most sense when it accompanies the procession of the catechumens to the baptistery.

Some songs, such as the processional *Nous venons vers toi* ("We come to you" A 21-87), combine the litany and the strophic form with refrain. This yields a richer musical development.*

Some songs structured on the pattern refrain-verse-refrain have been created as processionals, for example, the *Gloire à toi, Jésus* ("Glory to you, Jesus" MNA 82-15) for the procession of lights on February 2.

The litanic form works wells with any procession of either the whole assembly, part of the assembly, or a procession of ministers only.

2. *Troparion.* We class as *troparia* the chants in processional form we have inherited from Syrian *onyatha,* Byzantine antiphons or Latin introits. The Gregorian introit has come down to us in a simplified form: an antiphon is followed by a single verse and the doxology, then the antiphon is repeated. Originally, however, these pieces were developed for processions in which two choirs alternated singing the antiphon, psalmists sang the verses, and, in some instances, the congregation sang a refrain.

After the conciliar reform, when it was necessary to recreate vernacular forms of song in which the assembly could participate, the form of the *troparion* was proposed. It consisted of a stanza[27] for the choir, a refrain for the assembly and verses sung by cantors.[28] This proposal went nowhere until the Cistercian Francophone Commission began to offer texts for each Sunday and feast.[29] These texts elicited some musical creations; a few of these are beginning to find their way into parishes (for example, MNA 45.11 to 45.15).

This form is of interest for an ordinary entrance procession because of the richness of its three constituent elements and their interaction. (a) The stanza sets out the mystery and leads into prayer in the refrain. The verses develop the meaning of the *troparion* and move into the refrain. In a final reprise of the stanza we ponder its message more fully. (b) Three styles of music are used:

---

* James Hansen has worked to develop English forms of the litany for processions. His collection *Litany: When the Church Gathers* (Portland, OR: Oregon Catholic Press, 1986) contains "The Great Sunday Entrance Litany," in the classic style, and a litany with refrain of this type, "Litany for the Sick." – Editor

[27] The word "stanza" (French, "stance," from the Italian "stanza," "waiting room," is chosen because it corresponds to the Greek and Syriac words used for "verses" and meaning "little house."

[28] See the special issue of *Eglise qui Chante,* number 71-72; "Les chants processionaux." On the first troparia in French see *La Maison-Dieu* 96.

    This form has not been an element of English liturgical music. The only example that comes to mind that approximates this form is the setting of the Revelation 19:1-7 canticle by Howard Hughes. – Editor

[29] *Tropaires des dimanches,* Éd. SODEC, 1980.

verbo-melodism in the stanza, recitative in the verses, and choral in the refrain. (c) Three interpretive poles are in dialogue: the schola in the stanza, the assembly in the refrain, and the cantors on the verses. Before long the assembly is also able to join in singing the stanza.

Compared to the litany, the *troparion* with its refrains and verses provides a richer and more varied textual treatment of the mystery. But its more complex structure is also more demanding to perform.

3. Song with refrain. The song with refrain is without a doubt the most widely used form for the entrance song. It was almost the only form available when vernacular languages were introduced into the liturgy. It is also the easiest to use and the most popular.

    The alternating structure of a dialogue between the choir or cantors singing the verses and the assembly singing the refrain enables the assembly as a whole to enter into the movement of the opening procession and gives it meaning in itself.

    Obviously not every song makes a good entrance song. Those responsible must choose carefully so that the overall style of the song, its text and its music match the rite, the feast and the assembly. Some good examples would be *Aube nouvelle* ("New Dawn" MNA 31-51) or *Tenons en éveil* ("Keep Watch" MNA 47.25).*

    While I would not exclude them *a priori*, two further forms of song (4. and 5. below) do not adjust as well to the entrance rite because they are more static, more stational than processional.

4. Strophic Hymn. Among these I would include the strophic hymn that is stational by nature. Whether standing or seated, the entire assembly offers its praise by giving voice to a text that is carried by its music. Singing a hymn is a rite in itself, as, for instance, at the beginning of the Liturgy of the Hours and after communion. Doing anything else at the same time would be distracting.

    Some strophic songs that are more symbolic than meditative or prophetic lend themselves well to a procession. One example would be *Puisque Dieu nous a aimés* (MNA 82-84), which was originally a Gallican sequence for a procession.**

---

* In English, examples abound: Bob Hurd's "Gather Your People," and Marty Haugen's "All Are Welcome" are two songs that meet the criteria set out by Fr. Gelineau. – Editor

** Many public domain hymns, such as "All People That on Earth Do Dwell" set to the Old Hundredth tune, fit this category. – Editor

5. Other Sacred Music. Most pieces of sacred music, whether or not they use liturgical texts, are fragments designed to be sung for their own sake: airs, lieder, melodies, motets, excerpts from cantatas, and so on. If used at the beginning of Mass, they become a kind of musical overture to or background music for a festive procession. In some cases, particularly when the assembly does not join in the singing, this can be an interesting solution.

The same can be said of instrumental introductions (organ, brass ensemble, and so forth) in similar situations.

THE PROCESSION OF THE BOOK

In the Eastern rites, the Liturgy of the Word opens with an entrance procession in which the book is carried. Song accompanies the procession.

In the Roman liturgy the book is carried in the entrance procession,[30] but the cross, candles and incense are already part of this procession. The accumulation of symbols can keep us from appreciating each one. What we have already said about the cross in the entrance procession can also be said about the book.

Experience shows that the entrance of the book, carried high by the reader who passes through the assembly and goes up to the ambo while the assembly sings a song such as "Glory to you, Christ, Word...Wisdom...Light!" elicits great pastoral and liturgical interest. The piece reminds us that this is not only about a book, but also about Christ himself, the word of the Father.[31]

This song prepares the faithful to actively listen to the reading as the word of God and to welcome the message of salvation. When the song is finished and the lector opens her or his mouth, all eyes are on him or her, as they were on Jesus himself in the synagogue at Nazareth (cf. Luke 4:20). The first words are not lost, as we so often see.

---

[30] If there is a deacon and a book of the gospels, there is nothing to prevent him joining the entrance procession as long as the lectionary is carried in before the first reading.

[31] Let me tell of my own experience as a pastor of five parishes for 18 years. We processed in this way every Sunday at all the Masses, with the whole assembly singing the acclamation, *Gloire au Christ* ("Glory to Christ" MNA 21-11) by heart. If we didn't do it, it seemed like something was missing. It was as though someone had removed one of the steps leading up to the ambo. (The word "ambo" comes from the word *anabainô, which* means "to go up.")

　　There seems to be no parallel composition in English, but it would be like taking the Richard Proulx Lenten acclamation for the Gospel, "Glory to you, O Word of God, Lord Jesus Christ!" and repeating it using the words "Wisdom" and "Light" in place of "Word." – Editor

Given that it is optional to have the lectionary in the entrance procession (GIRM 82, "who may carry"),* and that nothing prohibits what can heighten our awareness of the word of God, there is no reason to *not* use this rite that our Eastern-rite brothers and sisters have been using for so long.

THE GOSPEL PROCESSION

As things are currently done, the gospel acclamation (the alleluia or whatever replaces it during Lent) can be seen as an acclamation if it is sung, but it is rarely done as a processional.

If the ambo is simply a lectern set in the sanctuary close to the altar, if it is only a few steps away and there are no steps to climb, if the priest or deacon who reads the gospel approaches the ambo empty-handed, without holding the book of the gospels or the lectionary where all can see it, if the verse is read, if the optional incensing is omitted, if the faithful are not caught up in a sense of anticipation and if they stand only when they hear "The Lord be with you," then nothing here really suggests a processional. What elements of this rite are worth keeping?

First, a processional needs a certain fullness. A short alleluia that lasts only a few seconds, followed by a spoken verse that interrupts the movement of the song, does not sufficiently highlight our preparation for the Good News, which we proclaim and listen to while standing.

A series of embodied ritual elements comes together to emphasize the importance of the rite of the gospel: the deacon's request for the priest's blessing, the minister's prayer as he bows toward the altar, the act of taking the book from the altar,[32] the gesture of accompanying the book with candles and incense. These elements are not obligatory and it is not always possible to use them. We must choose what is appropriate and what speaks to this specific assembly.

In this ritual moment the alleluia is a jubilant, grand acclamation, repeated immediately in whole or in part by the assembly, which is already on its feet. One or more verses are chanted by a cantor or a schola, leading back to a repetition of the alleluia by everyone.[33]

---

*The newly published IGMR 2002 #120 (d) refers to an "evangelarium" and prohibits the use of a lectionary. – Editor

[32] Few parishes are able to buy a book of the gospels, but many have two lectionaries. One can be placed on the altar to be used for the proclamation of the gospel. If this is not the case, the reader who proclaimed the last reading can simply place the lectionary on the altar. The priest or deacon can pick it up there at the beginning of the gospel procession.

[33] We need musically written verses. A simple psalm tone often seems too thin in this context unless it is harmonized. The *"Celtic Alleluia" by Christopher Walker addresses this need.* – Editor

The word "alleluia," which we have retained from the Hebrew, means "Praise God." In Gregorian chant, it occasioned expansive vocalizations by cantors. If these melodies are too difficult for the assembly, you can have them repeat the word "Alleluia" to extend the melody of the song. Harmonies also work beautifully.

During the seasons when we do not sing the alleluia, the lectionary offers verses structured in the same way: acclamation-verse-acclamation. These call for the same type of composition.

THE PROCESSION WITH THE GIFTS

Whereas the GIRM gives four functions for the entrance song, the same document (50) mentions only that a song accompanies the procession with the gifts. It simply indicates that the rules are the same as those for the entrance song. But it gives neither text for nor example of an offertory antiphon. It indicates only that it should last "at least until the gifts are placed on the altar" (GIRM 50), which indicates its processional role.

The only source for the offertory antiphon to which the conciliar reform could turn was the Gregorian Antiphonary, where the antiphon in question had no direct relationship with the Eucharist, but accompanied the collection of gifts among the faithful or, as in Rome, among the leading citizens. In contrast, in the Missal of Paul VI the song is clearly designated as accompanying the offering, especially the bread and wine that will be used in the Eucharist.

But if the GIRM says nothing about the content and texts of the offertory antiphons, it describes in detail the preparation rites that the song accompanies: how to prepare the altar table and lay out the table cloth, how the faithful bring the bread and wine to the ministers who place them on the table, and so on. Other gifts can be brought forward, but are not placed on the altar. The scene is well set for gestures (GIRM 49), but not for appropriate song.

The Texts

While we do not have a model either of the content of the text of the offertory song or of its musical form, we do have a precious witness to this song as the opening of the Lord's supper in the former Western and Eastern liturgies. This is particularly the case of the Byzantine liturgy where this song is called "the Great Entrance," in contrast to the "Little Entrance," that of the Book. We enter into the eucharistic action through the Lord's first gesture at the Last Supper: "he took the bread; he took the cup of wine," and we embark on his paschal journey with him. The text of the song called the *Cherubikon* compares

the people whose gifts are being offered to the cherubim who escort Christ as
he offers himself to the Father:

> Let us who mystically represent the cherubim
>
> and sing the thrice-holy hymn to the life-giving Trinity
>
> now lay aside all cares of life
>
> that we may welcome the king of all escorted invisibly
>
> by ranks of angels.
>
> Alleluia, alleluia, alleluia.

This is a far cry from the offertory hymns of the dialogue masses of the 1930s
and 1940s when we offered God the fruit of our own work. So what steps can we
take to bring this song to the foreground in the spirit of the Missal of Paul VI?

During the 1950s a song entitled *Toi seul est saint* ("You alone are holy"
MNA 25-11) appeared. Inspired by the *Cherubikon*, its text and its music are
still contemporary:

> He takes our poor gifts and fills them,
>
> He gives himself over into our hands to be our offering
>
> And in his church's Eucharist
>
> He offers us with himself to the Father....

It is a true processional. Verses for the soloist alternate with the assembly's refrain. The verses, which speak of what we are doing in the rite, truly accompany
the gesture of offering. We are escorting the King of the world in his passage to
the Father; the whole people accompanies him, offering themselves through his
gifts, and thus preparing themselves for the great eucharistic prayer of praise.*

After the Council, several texts of *troparia* for the offertory were proposed
(LMD 96), but as I mentioned earlier, almost no one responded. Most people
said, "At the offertory we sit down and rest. We listen to the organ. In due course
we respond 'Blessed be God for ever.' What else could anyone want?"

Music

What musical form would this restored chant take? If we analyze twenty
years' worth of creative activity, we can see that four forms are possible, each with
its own limits and possibilities.

---

* Because most English-speaking liturgists stress that the focus on offering is to come in the eucharistic prayer, there
are few good English examples of this style of text and music. – Editor

1. The model of the Byzantine *Cherubikon* is like a great antiphon in two parts. The first highlights adoration; the second, jubilation. It reminds me of the song *Don que Dieu fait aux hommes* ("God's Gift to Humanity"), based on Guerrero's wonderful tune. But this is a song in parts for a choir. With repeated usage, the assembly could certainly pick up a great antiphon in a unison setting, but no such thing has been attempted.

2. The easiest and most popular model is the song with verses and refrain, such as the song *Toi seul est saint* ("You Alone Are Holy" MNA 25-11). The text of the verses must always remain in the foreground, which happens in those assemblies that sing the verses by heart from beginning to end. This gives rise to a very strong sense that the church's action accompanies the presentation of the gifts.

3. The richest model for the rite in question is undoubtedly the *troparion*, with its stanza sung by the choir or by the whole assembly, the refrain sung by everyone, and the verses sung by soloists. These verses bring the assembly back into the refrain and the final reprise of the stanza, following the same pattern we saw for the entrance song. Such top-notch creations exist, just waiting for their quality to be recognized.[34]

The assembly will have to make some effort if it is going to adopt this form, but experience has shown that this is very worthwhile.

4. The strophic form of the chorale has been used to create good offertory hymns, either for choir, for example, *Parmi son peuple en fête* ("Among His Celebrating People," B54), or for assembly, whether adults or children such as *Préparons la table* ("Prepare the Table," B21.85).

By nature, the strophic hymn is not processional. If it is used for the offertory, its structure and its musical style need to keep pace with the slow steps of those who are carrying the offerings and with the interiorization that the rite envisages.

The vast majority of liturgical assemblies, whether they be large or small, have yet to discover the spiritual and liturgical value of the offertory procession in enabling the whole assembly to enter into the Eucharist.

But those who have done this regularly over several years can witness to the pastoral benefit derived from the "Great Entrance." The eucharistic prayer,

---

[34] In 1970 the French publishing house Desclée published *Neuf Offertoires* (Nine Offertory Hymns) by different composers, based on texts from the *Centre National de Pastorale Liturgique*. Almost as soon as they were published, the publisher scrapped them. Some are currently being reprinted.

which is the high point of the liturgy, becomes more communal, denser, and more responsive to the Spirit. In this way the first of the Lord's gestures at the Last Supper recovers its full meaning and all its mystical value. This rite forms a threshold: entry into the mystery, opening to praise, offering of the whole church.

THE COMMUNION PROCESSIONAL

Of all the sung parts of the Mass, it is the communion hymn whose antiquity is best demonstrated. Third-century hymn texts in lyrical prose, and fourth-century responsorial psalms, especially Psalm 33 with its refrain, "Taste and see that the Lord is good," point to its venerable age. The Gregorian Antiphonary has left us only one antiphon for the schola which was enough in an era when only the priest received communion.

In the 1950s, during the progress of the liturgical movement that would lead to Vatican II, the song during communion took root afresh as people once again began to receive communion during Mass, and the use of the vernacular at this part of the Mass was again permitted.

The reform of Vatican II restored the communion processional. Only rarely, however, is this song actually sung in France.

Functions

The GIRM (56i) assigns three functions to the communion song:

- "to express outwardly the communicants' union in spirit by means of the unity of their voices." The unique symbolism of the fusion of voices as the sign of the unity of those who are singing takes on a particularly clear meaning at the time of sacramental communion;

- to "give evidence of joy of heart." This is the joy of the wedding feast of the Lamb to which communicants are invited; and

- to "make the procession to receive Christ's body more fully an act of community." The song enhances the dignity, good order and cohesiveness of this collective gesture. From this it derives its processional nature.

Forms

The Sacramentary gives a proper text as the communion antiphon for each Mass. If these texts are going to be sung, most likely a schola will do the singing. But if you want the assembly to be able to sing the refrain, you can choose a simpler antiphon.

The responsorial form is best fitted to produce a song that will last throughout the whole communion. For example, you can alternate the antiphon or refrain with verses from a well-chosen psalm (Psalm 22, 33, 41, 62, and so on), sung by one or two soloists.

You might also use texts created for the procession. Some have a litanic form, such as *De la table du Seigneur* ("From the Lord's Table" MNA 29-13), based on a venerable ancient text. Some work with a verse-refrain form such as *Voici le pain* ("Here Is the Bread" MNA 29.30). Others use a simple strophic form such as *Nous qui mangeons le pain de la promesse* ("We Who Eat the Bread of the Promise" MNA 29.22), which people can learn by heart. A choir could also sing an appropriate motet. Lastly, you can decide on an organ piece or another instrumental piece.*

An Opportunity

Even though the song during communion was fairly well developed before Vatican II, it has lost ground since the conciliar reform. I believe there are two principal reasons for this:

1. One innovation of the Missal of Paul VI was to allow a hymn to be sung by the whole assembly after the silence after communion (GIRM 56j). We will look at the benefits of this hymn later. Assemblies that adopted this practice have found that having singing at the breaking of bread, and during and after communion, felt like overload. Therefore, a break during communion seemed desirable.

2. Not all communicants want to sing during this very personal journey to the minister who is distributing communion. This is even more evident after they have received communion and want to spend some time in recollection when they return to their places. This is felt all the stronger if they need to carry a book in order to sing the verses.

---

*English examples of psalms (especially psalm 34), songs with brief refrains and hymns for communion abound. The James E. Moore Psalm 34, "Taste and See," Suzanne Toolan's "I Am the Bread of Life," and Jerry Brubaker's "O Blessed Savior," and Omer Westendorf/Robert Kreutz's "Gift of Finest Wheat" are examples of this type. – Editor

Therefore, sometimes people prefer to emphasize the song accompanying the breaking of bread (we will examine its importance later) and the post-communion hymn, and leave the communion time in silence. You can play background music.

It is possible to have a communion hymn if there is a choir to lead the assembly or community in the communion hymn, especially if it has a refrain that everyone is free to sing if they wish.

3. In large celebrations where the rite of distribution of communion is complex and long, it could be good to use a grand *troparion*-litanic type processional such as *Si le Père vous appelle* ("If the Father Calls You" MNA 83.23-cf. 83.22 and 83.24) or chants built on an ostinato such as Taizé's *Il n'est pas de plus grand amour* ("There is No Greater Love").*

ABOUT THE CLOSING HYMN

On some occasions, such as after baptisms or ordinations, the Mass concludes with a procession. It is normal to accompany this departure with an appropriate song.

But at ordinary Masses, there is nothing to add after "Go in the peace of Christ." Why keep people back to sing another song? The closing hymn is a vestige of the old sung Latin Mass in which the only song in French was after Mass. Today it would be better to help assemblies discover the post-communion hymn, which is completely at home in the celebration.

---

* The custom of singing more than one hymn during the communion procession is a less desirable solution to this situation. "Eat This Bread" is the Taizé composition most associated with Communion in English. – Editor

CHAPTER 3

ACCLAMATIONS, PROCLAMATIONS AND DIALOGUES

We are not accustomed to counting the brief vocal actions, the acclamations and dialogues, among the sung parts of the Mass. However, they play an important role in the celebration.

First, there are many of them. In one celebration of the Eucharist it is possible to have between twenty and thirty interventions of this type. Second, they punctuate the celebration and structure it, particularly by opening and closing ritual units such as the opening, the gospel, the eucharistic action and the dismissal. Finally, they are, or should be, intense moments of participation by the assembly, manifesting and realizing its role as the first subject of liturgical action. Without them, we cannot fully "sing the Mass."

Acclamations

An acclamation is a collective vocal act that expresses admiration for, compliments or congratulates someone, or simply expresses the joy of a feast.

The content of the words we use is not the primary issue. For instance, just as in French we willingly use words that originate in other languages such as "*Vivat!*," "*Hurray!*" and "*Bravo!*" so in Christian liturgy we have kept Hebrew words such as "amen," "alleluia," "Hosanna" and "*Maranatha*," which make sense in the rites in which they are used.

Amen

"It's solid; it's true; we agree." "Amen" is the word the Bible uses to ratify the covenant between God and his people. It concludes significant moments in our celebrations:the end of the opening prayer, the general intercessions, the eucharistic prayer and the prayer after communion.

If we want to keep these amens from simply being mumbled or whispered, the very opposite of an acclamation, we need music that is closer to a shout than to a song. However, aside from exceptional situations of spontaneous collective enthusiasm, this exclamation is normally stylized, that is "ritualized," in the best sense of the word, allowing easy access to its meaning.

The melodies written for this music should naturally follow from the cantillation of the text that the amen concludes. These tones are generally very simple; they repeat the last note (A-A, for example), or the sub-tonic and tonic (G-A). This extreme simplicity permits a response that is easily sung as one voice.

But it is also possible to envisage settings of the amen that are more developed, such as that at the end of the "Through him, with him…" of the eucharistic prayer. Another possibility would be to prolong each consecration by a neume of adoration. Polyphony may be used if it does not destroy the acclamation's sense of unanimity but reinforces it by enriching it.

The amens that conclude the Glory to God or other songs are an integral part of these songs.

The Alleluia

The Hebrew word "alleluia," which means "praise God," is undoubtedly the most used acclamation in Christian worship. Most often it is integrated into a true song, such as in the case of the gospel procession where the acclamation is intensified by means of one or more verses that lead back into it.

The alleluia is also found at the end of some antiphons, particularly those for the Easter season. It is also incorporated into certain refrains or verses of hymns, or serves as the refrain.

Its major use is at the Easter Vigil, where it is sung three times, each time rising a tone. It is the shout *par excellence* of Easter victory.

The lovely sound of different vowels and the fluidity of consonants make "alleluia" an ideal word, not only for acclamations but also for jubilant vocalizations. This is in particular due to the resounding but contrasting resonances of the vowel sounds "ou" and "a." Given its malleability, the alleluia can be part of many kinds of song.

Glory to You, Lord! Praise to You, Lord Jesus Christ!

These two acclamations respond to the two exclamations chanted by the minister: "A reading from the gospel according to…" and "The gospel of the Lord."

Luckily the rhythm and phonetics of the French words, as well as the ritual melodies offered by the Sacramentary, are good. Unless the minister cannot sing, it would be unfortunate to remove from the celebration this strong sign of the assembly on its feet, acclaiming the Good News.

"For the Kingdom, the Power…."

After the Our Father and its embolism, "Deliver us, Lord from every evil," which have their own cantillations, the Lord's Prayer concludes with a powerful acclamation: "For the kingdom, the power and the glory are yours…." Since (in French) the spoken formula "For to you belong…." is not good for singing, the Sacramentary offered a more vigorous and sonorous alternative formulation, "To you, the Kingdom…." The suggested melody is good, but others, possibly harmonized, are conceivable.

The principal acclamations of the Mass are those belonging to the eucharistic prayer; the most important of all is the Holy, Holy. But the eucharistic prayer is made up of elements that must be treated as a whole. Its dialogue, proclamation, cantillation, and acclamations will be addressed in Chapter 6.

ANNOUNCEMENTS

Comparative studies of liturgy show that ritual announcements are usually assigned to the deacon. The deacon sends off processions, invites people to stand or kneel, dismisses catechumens, declares that the celebration of the Eucharist is completed, and, above all, proclaims the intentions of the prayers of the faithful.

In the Roman church today, deacons rarely play a liturgical role in our assemblies. More often, the priest, a cantor or a lector takes care of diaconal announcements in different contexts such as the announcements that frame the gospel, the invitation to exchange the sign of peace, the opening of the prayer of the faithful and the final dismissal.

So that the assembly can sing its part, the music for these announcements is permanent and standardized. The Sacramentary provides settings that are generally well-suited to these announcements.

Vatican II restored the prayers of the faithful in a litanic form. We will look at them when we deal with litanies.

DIALOGUES

Each important part of the Mass (the opening, the gospel, the eucharistic prayer, the exchange of peace and the dismissal) opens with a dialogue between the presider and the assembly. It gets the ritual action going, or starts it up again, and facilitates the free, conscious and active participation of the entire assembly.

"The Lord Be with You" (*Dominus vobiscum*)

The traditional formula of this dialogue goes back to the origins of Christian worship: "The Lord be with you. And with your Spirit."

The words "The Lord (is/be/will be)[35] with you" run through the whole Bible. In their own way, they constantly restate God's promise to his people. "Through his greeting the priest declares to the assembled community that the Lord is present" (GIRM 28).

"This greeting and the congregation's response express the mystery of the gathered church" (GIRM 28). Unadorned words cannot begin to capture the profound truth and real importance of this brief exchange. Chanting gives it more fullness and meaning. The tones proposed by the Sacramentary are as easy as they are traditional.

The words "And with your spirit," taken from 1 Corinthians 2:10, do not mean simply "Hey, you too" as one might say in a polite, but informal exchange. They mean that "he who presides should receive in his spirit (*esprit*) the gift of the Spirit that corresponds to his function" (*Dans Vos Assemblées*, 372). This is significant. It is good to help the faithful understand this and also remember that the priest cannot celebrate without the presence and consent of the participants.

The Missal of Paul VI provides several other biblical greetings for the opening dialogue, along with appropriate responses. Here again, the suggested music corresponds well to the rite.

---

[35] In Hebrew as in Latin, the formula has no verb. The tense remains undetermined. Since a verb is necessary in French, the optative "be" is used to translate this opening.

The most important and best-developed dialogue of the Mass is found at the beginning of the eucharistic prayer. It will be addressed when we look at the eucharistic prayer.

A final reminder just before the last blessing and the dispersal of the assembly is also a dismissal: "The Lord be with you on your journey."

All these dialogues tie the celebrating assembly together. These are not crumbs to brush away or rites to observe in a formalist manner. Rather, these exchanges awaken our consciousness of truly being the church formed in serving the Lord in the liturgy.

Chapter 4

CANTILLATIONS

Within the resonant universe of Christian worship, we have distinguished two categories of ritual music: cantillation, in which the rhythmic and melodic movement depends on the proper delivery of words; and songs, properly speaking, in which rhythm and melody are the engines of the musical action.

Now, within the body of Christian liturgies, cantillation far outnumbers songs. This priority results from the predominant role of the word in Christian worship, based first on the reading of scripture and the preaching of the gospel to which the baptized respond with thanksgiving and petitions.

Biblical readings, in particular the psalms, the prefaces and various prayers, of which the most eminent is the Our Father, are also classified as cantillations. The types of cantillation vary according to the literary genre of the text to be chanted and according to how the text is ritually situated within the liturgical action as a whole.

By its nature, cantillation is the action of a soloist who is the minister of a rite. It might be a lector, a presider singing a preface or a prayer, a deacon proclaiming prayer intentions, a cantor singing the verses of a psalm. Only an individual can fully put before the assembly the true sense of the spoken word. Some exceptions do exist, however; for example, congregational psalmody made possible by poetic structure of verses, and the Our Father.

We will deal with psalmody, readings, prefaces, presidential prayers, and the Our Father. The creed will be dealt with in a section at the end of this chapter.

THE PSALM

The psalm is one of the four biblical passages—Old Testament reading, psalm, epistle and gospel—of which the Liturgy of the Word for Sundays and feasts is normally composed.

The psalm's uniqueness in relationship to the other readings is immediately apparent. Most of the other readings are situated in the history of salvation and refer to historical events and people. Psalms, on the other hand, are poems. Even if they allude to historical events, their literary genre is that of poetry. By nature, poetry is not closed in to the time it was created, but can be heard by people as a message directed to them in the here and now: "O that today you would listen to his voice...." "To you, O Lord, I lift up my soul," "I will praise you, Lord, for you have rescued me." Each time they are read, the words of the psalm of the day say something new to each person.

The Evolution of the Psalm

Over the centuries the psalm of the Mass has assumed several different forms. During the first centuries of Christianity, it seems to have been treated as another biblical reading in the Liturgy of the Word.

During the fourth and fifth centuries, the responsorial form appeared. A psalmist chanted the verses and the whole assembly responded by a refrain that used words taken from the psalm.

By the seventh to eighth centuries, the people no longer joined in the songs. Cantors expanded the melodies of the earlier responses while the lone remaining verse was executed in very ornate form by the psalmist, who sang from one of the steps (*gradus*) of the ambo, from which the name "gradual" was given to this psalm.

The rediscovery of the psalms was one of the fruits of the pre- and post-conciliar liturgical renewal. The psalm as a psalm was restored to the Liturgy of the Word after the first reading. The lectionary presents it in responsorial form; its refrain is taken from the psalm, and selected verses are entrusted to the psalmist or lector.

Thanks to the books and leaflets containing the psalm of the day that people use more and more frequently, each person can now not only sing the refrain, but can also ponder the inspired word that the whole assembly sings in the psalm.

In light of our considerations in this chapter, we will examine the sung refrain and chanted verses separately.

The Refrain

As we normally know it, the psalm refrain, sometimes called the antiphon, does not derive from cantillation, but from verbo-melodism and, sometimes, even from the chorale form. Normally it has its own melodic shape and a measured rhythm that is derived from the text. This is why it can be detached from the verses.

However, in true responsorial psalmody, such as that which existed in Judaism and in certain parts of the Mediterranean basin during the first centuries of Christianity, or which can be heard today in some African chants, the response is so inseparable from the verses of the psalms that they form a single unit. This is particularly the case in the alleluiatic psalms. Here the alleluia is a response integrated into the rhythm of the psalmody. The response returns frequently and quickly, at the end of each stich,* which normally corresponds to a written line. This psalmody, which demands a major investment by the group that is celebrating, is rare in our assemblies (see Lucien Deiss' *Louez serviteurs du Seigneur, alleluia....* "Praise, servants of the Lord, alleluia....").**

Verses

The verses are sung on chanting tones that are appropriate for the poetic structure of the psalm and the modality of the refrain. A psalmist normally chants the verses from the ambo or an equivalent spot. Two psalmists who work well together can sing the psalm in two parts.

To make things easier, the lectionary usually offers only extracts from the chosen psalm that relate to the readings. These verses are almost always set out in four-line strophes that are ordinarily the equivalent of two verses from the text. This encourages using the refrain after each four-line strophe.

Looking at Experience

After more that thirty years of using the responsorial psalm in the Mass, several questions deserve some reflection. First, not every assembly has adopted the responsorial psalm as such. Some replace it with a song.

Some claim that repeating the refrain after each strophe leads to a kind of weariness. In true responsorial psalmody, there is no break between the stich and the response and the return to the stich. It is one seamless act, lively and dynamic, that holds the assembly in the experience of the sung psalm. In our system of refrains, there is a break between the verse and the refrain. Each time the psalmody has to be kick-started again, which is tiring and tedious.

---

* A *verse* is made up of several parts (often equivalent to a line of text) called "stichs." – Translator
** In English, settings of the Canticle from Daniel 3 (including Gelineau's own) are examples of this form. – Editor

The verse, the basic poetic structure of the psalm, is no longer seen as such. Rather, it is absorbed into the strophe.

In response to the four-line layout, people choose or write four-phrase psalm tones that cover the whole strophe.* These tones abandon the basic principle of psalmody, of reciting the whole stich on the chanting tone, with cadences in the middle and at the end of the verse. The chanting tone is not intended to express the emotions of the text. In contrast, where the melody is written by strophe, it tends to change the reciting note from one verse to the next. Often the ups and downs of the melody misinterpret the text.[36]

Except in those cases where short psalms are used in their entirety, cutting the stichs and reworking them into strophes often distort the poem.

Using the psalms each week should instill key formulas of revealed faith in the spirit and heart. While some refrains stick in the memory and nourish prayer, it seems that the texts of the psalms are still foreign to those who come to hear the word. Unlike the Fathers of the Church who explained to the people the psalms they sang, homilists today rarely use the psalms in their homilies.

When the Congregation Sings the Psalm

GIRM 36 describes alternating between verses sung by a soloist and the refrain sung by all as the ordinary way of performing the psalm, but other choral or spoken forms are not excluded. This includes having the whole assembly sing the psalm.

By singing the entire psalm, some assemblies have discovered that they can "chew on" and be nourished by the bread of the psalm's word. They rediscover the psalm's basic structure through the verses. It is good to alternate verses between a soloist and everyone, or between two choirs. The psalm is recited or chanted calmly; the mediant cadences and the balance between the lines are respected carefully. The chant uses very simple tones of few notes. The psalm continues until its singing has established a real period of contemplation.

This does not mean that the refrain of the day is not used. The text of the refrain is actually an interpretive key that links the different readings. Rather than being sung every fourth line, the refrain can be sung at the beginning, in the middle and at the end of the psalm.

It's easy to see from this why selecting more verses than the Lectionary gives would be attractive. The psalm regains its meaning. Above all, it washes over and

---

* Stichs make up verses; several verses make a strophe. In translating *strophique*, the word "strophic" was used when it referred to a repeated musical pattern or a repeated textual and musical pattern. – Translator

[36] For psalm technique, see J. Gelineau, "Traité de psalmodie," in *Eglise qui chante*, 22.

through the assembly in waves, establishing a time of contemplation that is very precious for prayer. There is no other rite like this in the Mass. It is a time to relax the brain and savor the Word that gradually penetrates our understanding, is fixed in our memories, and re-emerges as spontaneous prayer.

Listening to an Inspired Poem

Another way of letting the psalm speak to our hearts is by listening to it read slowly by a single voice, like a poem. No refrain is used. This reading allows us to understand different things than we would if we were reading it with our own eyes or singing it ourselves.

This poetic reading can be done over a background of music played on the organ or guitar. But use your judgment; this approach wears thin quickly.

Florid Chant

We must not neglect florid cantillation, of the kind that typified what the psalm had become in Gregorian chant. This is yet another musical and contemplative approach to the psalm. It presupposes real creations of high musical quality, and very few examples of this exist in French. It also presupposes cantors who have the requisite technique.

In conclusion, note that using only one way of performing the psalm in the Mass can become routine. These inspired poems, so rich and varied, will better strike a chord in us if we vary the forms of psalmody and the musical genres we use.

THE BIBLICAL READINGS

The Tone of Public Discourse

In every culture, public speech uses certain tones and rhythms: the tone of the town crier, the *cursus* of the Latin orators, the alexandrines of classical tragedy, and so on. This tone depends on the messenger's authority, the context in which the message is promulgated, the relationship between messenger and listeners, the acoustics of the place, and so on.

The widespread use of narrow-casted, individualized communication by the media (microphones, loudspeakers, telephones, radios, televisions, etc.) has flattened the tone of public communication. Instead of one person speaking to listeners in an appropriate tone from the podium, from the stage, from the pulpit or wherever, people who speak into the microphone most often speak as if they were addressing each person personally and each radio or television listener receives the message individually. Dramatic or professorial tones now seem out of place because they seem inappropriately solemn.

On some occasions people still spontaneously adopt a tone appropriate to the circumstance, for example when proposing a toast, at funerals, and during solemn ceremonies. But in terms of the liturgy, the question of tone still remains.

If the person who preaches at the microphone uses a preaching tone, it quickly seems ridiculous. But, on the other hand, if the presider speaks a preface in the ordinary tone of private conversation, there is a rift between the action of speaking and the ritual situation. The same applies to the words of the consecration. When the presider is using a microphone, he needs to speak in the voice he would use when the microphone is off. The authenticity of the rite calls for agreement among the ritual act, what is said, and the assembly that is present.

Reading Sacred Scripture

Among all ritual words, the reading of sacred scripture has a special status. It is proclaimed to be heard as the word of God. It is read from a special book, the Bible, using a canonical formula that the reader may not change. Each listener ought to be able to receive this word according to each one's heart and the Spirit's desires. Therefore readers must not impose on the sacred text their own intellectual or emotional interpretation by their intonations or the inflections of their voice. Certainly they must invest themselves as fully as possible in the act of reading, even as they constantly listen first to what is being said, and try to fulfill as much as possible their role of passing on the word by their voice and their whole person.

Here the question of tone comes in. In Jewish tradition, it is said that whoever reads the Bible without cantillating it is an idolater. He or she fails to indicate that what they are proclaiming is not their own word, but God's. Thus, whoever cantillates the Hebrew text must do two things. First, they follow the special signs in the written text that indicate how phrases are formed and where stresses in the words should be placed so that listeners can grasp the accurate meaning of what is said. Second, the same annotations indicate where the voice should be modulated so that the tone does not become a melody or an air, but underlines the meaning of the text. The tone is both conventional and understandable, neutral and meaningful.

All Christian liturgical traditions have handed down tones adapted to their own language and to the culture in which they were born. Thus the Roman liturgy had in Latin a tone for the epistle, a tone for the gospel, a tone for the Lamentations, and so on. What is happening with this in French today?

With the adoption of the vernacular after Vatican II, there was a preference for using the tone of ordinary spoken communication to make it easier for people to understand the biblical texts that had just been introduced into the Lectionary, and which were, for the most part, unknown. The question of reading tones for the Bible was simply set aside.

This question differs greatly from language to language and culture to culture. It seems that French is very particular in this regard. Delivery may be elegant and good, be it in a solemn or more intimate setting, but it is to be flat, with few inflections. This is especially true of poetry. A tone seems to be a superfluous, useless, even bothersome, embellishment. When lectors repeat a conventional tone for each phrase, they neutralize the meaning instead of affirming it, and compromise the transmission of the sacred word. A sing-song style of delivery can have the same effect.

In these circumstances, is it still possible to say that cantillating biblical readings in French has a purpose? Would it always seem to be a useless, even undesirable, embellishment?

Its value can nonetheless be seen in certain situations. For example, the gospel of the resurrection at the Easter Vigil or that of the birth of Christ at Christmas midnight Mass deserves a festive cantillation. In contrast, during a celebration of the Liturgy of the Hours, reading the word of God in a meditative and introspective manner, without spontaneous inflections, in a relatively flat tone except for a few inflections at the end, already constitutes a true ritual tone.

Our public reading of the scriptures remains, most often, too intellectual in that it does not get beyond a literal initial reading of the text. It is not open enough to what lies beyond the mystery to which the inspired Word calls us. It can impede the free and unpredictable action of the Holy Spirit. It is missing the air, in both senses of the word, that cantillation would bring to it.

Neither our so-called modern culture, nor our French language, nor our lack of openness to mysticism can render the question of tones for biblical readings anachronistic. Without a generalized solution, the question remains. There are still so many ritual behaviors to recreate! The central issue of biblical readings cannot be dismissed.

PREFACES

The lyrical summit of the Mass is found in the preface that opens each eucharistic prayer. The assembly has just given its assent: "It is right to give him thanks and praise." Now the presider proclaims the wonderful works that God has done for the human race.

The balanced phrases of the literary structure of the text are already lyrical. The French translations of the original Latin texts have preserved this style of rhythmic proclamation.

The Sacramentary provides a chant tone that is a plausible adaptation of the Latin tone with its four notes that can be so easily memorized. However, today's ear, accustomed as it is to the current dominant major/minor tonality, tends to hear the final bars of each chanted unit in a minor key. By borrowing the soh-la-ti-do ending of Greco-Byzantine tones, several of the recently published prefaces for the feasts of the Blessed Virgin Mary brighten this moment of praise.

A bright and lyrically spoken proclamation is always acceptable, but chant, well done, more clearly indicates that we are entering into the Eucharist as praise.

THE PRESIDENTIAL PRAYERS

Four times in the Mass a presidential prayer concludes a ritual unit: at the end of the opening rites, at the end of the general intercessions, at the end of the presentation of the gifts, and after communion.

Both the binary structure ("You who... do...") and the rhythmic cursus of the final phrases of the Latin originals of many of these prayers show that these texts used a special reciting tone. They also show that from a particular point in time they were set to chanting tones that have been passed down to us.

A good number of the prayers from the Sacramentary work fairly well with the traditional tone adjusted for French. To achieve this, presiders must avoid a monotonously syllabic delivery and respect punctuation according to meaning. Because proper chanting slows down delivery and highlights good phrasing, the text of these prayers, which is often very dense, can become more intelligible.

It seems that we must avoid two extremes. We must not systematically reject the practice of chanting the presidential prayers, which in many instances can emphasize them. We must not insist on singing every prayer, since the texts may not lend themselves to it or the context of the assembly may not call for it.

Still on this point, cultural and liturgical developments can modify how we chant and our perception of it.

THE OUR FATHER

In the Mass, the Lord's Prayer is a unique verbal act. Its origin is not simply inspired scripture, but the Lord's own lips. It lies at the heart of the Eucharist. The balanced rhythm of its three hopes and four petitions reminds us of the psalms.

The Lord's Prayer is not one of the "sung parts of the Mass." It should remain what it is, the prayer that belongs to the whole Christian assembly. Reciting it slowly, meditatively, quietly is a very good way of saying this prayer during Mass.

But its balanced text also lends itself well to being sung, if it is chanted in a subdued manner and if melody does not take on a life of its own that inevitably interferes with the text.[37] The official tone given in the French missal is a good chant tone, but not everyone can grasp its B mode. Fortunately there are other possibilities to choose from.

A setting with several parts can also be good if it does not keep people from participating in the prayer and if it respects the spirit of the prayer, for example, Rimsky-Korsakov's setting or that of Xavier Darasse.

THE PROFESSION OF FAITH

In Search of Its Status

The Nicene Creed is not one of the fundamental elements of the eucharistic liturgy. It was introduced into different liturgies between the sixth and ninth centuries as a reminder of orthodox faith at a time when the eucharistic prayer, the most elevated profession of Christian faith, was no longer heard or understood.

In the East, the symbol or profession of faith was recited by the deacon before the anaphora. In Spain, it was said before communion. In German-speaking countries in the ninth century, it followed the gospel. Its chant form probably originated in Greek communities of southern Italy. *Credos* I and II of the Gregorian repertoire show us that this cantillation had a single melodic formula, composed of two or three phrases that are adapted to each successive phrase of the text. Then it was sung by the schola. It came to Rome in the eleventh century.

---

[37] In the sense that all expressive melody becomes part of the interpretation of the text.

In the Latin West, the creed became one of the masterworks of the sung Mass for choir directors and choirs. Thanks to the plainchant Masses of Du Mont, it also became a popular song for festive gatherings, in particular since the end of the 17th century.

The reform of Vatican II shook up this state of affairs. The Missal of Paul VI kept the creed after the homily to "serve[s] as a way for the people to respond and to give their assent to the Word of God heard in the readings and through the homily, and for them to call to mind the truths of faith before they begin to celebrate the eucharist" (GIRM 43). It is said or sung by the priest with the people (GIRM 44).

But what happens in practice? Among the hundreds of French settings of the ordinary of the Mass, there are few settings of the creed, and they are almost never used in parishes. The creed is recited, often in a boring, lifeless way. Sometimes sung acclamations are inserted into it.

Furthermore, after listening to the word, we look forward to the prayers that flow from it in the General Intercessions. Reciting the creed often seems to break this momentum by cutting short the echo of the word within us. Finally, the richness of the proclamation of faith during the celebration, in the readings, the preaching, and the prayers make the necessity of reciting the creed each Sunday less evident. It would have more of an impact if it were spoken or sung on occasions that would highlight it.

Current Usage

Although the creed's ritual roots are too obscure to let us deduce any musical form specific to it, we can examine several current usages.

The Nicene Creed is a page of conciliar theology that has been translated into French with little lyricism. Among existing compositions, we can however find settings, for example AL 2, that some assemblies could use.

In France use of the Apostles' Creed is permitted, and is the most-used text because it is simpler and shorter. But this summary of baptismal catechesis also lacks lyricism. Different settings, such as *Je crois en Dieu* ("I believe in God") by Lucien Deiss exist.*

The only text of liturgical origin is the baptismal profession of faith, which we have in the question-and-answer form used at the Easter vigil and in baptism.

---

*No English version of the creed is used widely enough to be considered a parallel to these references. – Editor

It is a very good text for the assembly's song. As in the Byzantine liturgy, it can begin with "we believe," which is more normal (for example, MNA 23.31).

To obtain better participation by the assembly in our common profession of faith, composers have attempted a certain number of responsorial settings. A soloist sings the sections of the text concerning the Father, the Son and the Holy Spirit; each is followed by an acclamation such as *Je crois, Seigneur, mais augmente ma foi!* ("I believe, Lord, but deepen my faith!" MNA 23.22. The original is in L79).

I can envision a *faux-bourdon* setting of any of the three texts cited. This form would work well with a choir, but can rarely be sung by the whole assembly.

CHAPTER 5

LITANIES

VARIOUS LITANIC FORMS

The word "litany" comes from the Greek *litê*, meaning "prayer." The same term is used both for different types of processions, especially long penitential processions, and the type of repetitive song that accompanies them.

The most typical model of litanic song in the Latin tradition is found in the litanies of the saints sung in the Greater Litanies on April 25 at the feast of St. Mark during the Easter season, and the Lesser Litanies of the three rogation days before Ascension. They are still sung at ordinations and a shortened form is sung during the Easter vigil to accompany the procession to the baptistry.

The litanies of the saints are a motley group indicating the variety of forms the word "litany" can designate. There is, however, one basic model: an invocation sung by cantors to which the assembly responds with a prayer of supplication.

There are no less than six different forms in the litanies of the saints:[38]

- 1st section: the initial *Kyrie*. Immediately everyone repeats the invocations that the cantors began: *Kyrie... Christe...* and so on, for nine invocations.

- 2nd section: Invocations of the saints (64 names or titles) to which the response is, "Pray for us." This is the most typical form, and the one we generally think of when we speak of a litany. It has

---

[38] If you do not have the original Latin or Gregorian chant, you can find the equivalent of each section in MNA, respectively in numbers 34.84, 65.18, 33-13 and 33-31.

been used as a model for the litanies of the Blessed Virgin Mary, of the Sacred Heart, and so on.

- 3rd section, part A: Twelve penitential intercessions to be free from all types of evil, to which the response is, "Lord, save your people."

- 3rd section, part B: Using the same format and the same music, ten invocations *by* the mysteries of Christ, with the same response, "Lord, save your people."

- 4th section: After three penitential invocations comes a real set of general intercessions, with thirteen intentions. These are more developed than in earlier sections. The response is "We beseech you, hear us."

- 5th section: A triple Lamb of God with various responses and a concluding melody after the third invocation.

- 6th and 7th sections: After two choirs sing Psalm 69 antiphonally comes a series of verses alternating between the cantor and everyone.

Thus the litanies of the saints provide five variations on a basic model.

IN THE MASS

Three ordinary sung parts of the Mass are built on the litanic form: the Lord have mercy, the Lamb of God and the prayers of the faithful.

None of these is a processional, but as we have indicated in studying the entrance hymn, the extended litany was a privileged form for accompanying a more solemn and festive entrance. This same form can also be adapted and used in certain communion processionals.

Whether or not sacramental rites are involved, this can also be the case in some rites celebrated during Mass in which movement from place to place is involved: baptism, confirmation, profession of faith, weddings, and so on.

The litanic form provides for song that lasts a long time without tiring the singers. It lets everyone participate readily by addressing words of prayer directly to God, rather than being a commentary on God.

Let us now look at the three litanies of the Mass that are not processionals.

The Lord Have Mercy

Unless this invocation was already used in the penitential rite, the Lord Have Mercy begins at the end of the penitential rite. Because in the Lord Have Mercy the faithful both acclaim the Lord and implore his mercy, it is usually sung by all, the people and a choir or cantor, each with their own part.

Each acclamation is normally repeated twice, but that does not exclude it from being repeated more frequently, depending on the idiom of different languages, the music or other circumstances. A short verse may also be interpolated between acclamations (GIRM 30).

How to understand it

If the origins of the *Kyrie* in the Roman Mass are obscure, so is the interpretation of its ritual roots. Scholars have suggested three origins:

1. It is the vestige of an opening litany similar to those of various Eastern and Western rites but it has lost its intercessions.

2. It is a trace of an ancient Prayer of the Faithful that had already disappeared by the time of St. Gregory the Great. The invocation-response element had been conserved, and moved back before the readings. Its melodic form developed over the centuries.

3. It is a triple invocation addressed to Christ by the cantors, specific to the beginning of the Mass.

The Missal of Paul VI offers us two possible lines of interpretation.

1. "Praising the Lord and imploring his mercy" (GIRM 30).

Here the Lord is designated as Christ, the glorious and merciful Christ whose image has just been placed before us in the processional cross.[39]

After the humbly and marvelously imploring forms of the ancient Gregorian *Kyries* (XVI and XVII), the melismatic developments that followed expressed in their own way a prayer that is both awe and supplication.

Currently each of the three invocations is sung twice, once by the cantors and once by everyone, or three times if the melody demands it.

Some polyphonic settings respect this interpretation very well. But if they are too elaborate, they can create an imbalance in the dynamic of the opening rites except during very solemn ceremonies.

---

[39] The Trinitarian interpretation of *Kyrie-Christe-Kyrie* is late; it appears only with the tropes of the Middle Ages. The GIRM did not keep it.

2.   Reintegrate a real litany into the penitential rite (GIRM 30).

Standing before Christ, we implore him; the cantors chant a short intention and the people respond with a simple prayer of supplication.

This format has already been tested in French-speaking countries and seems to respond to what people want. When the entrance procession and song are finished, and the presider has reverenced the cross and greeted the assembly,[40] we are ready to call on Christ, our Savior. For example:

Cantor: On your people who hope in your grace.

All: Have pity, O Lord, etc.[41]

- The intentions are not supposed to list our sins, but to proclaim our trust in Christ's mercy. Experience indicates that three to five short intentions work well.

- The refrain can be Lord have mercy/*Kyrie eleison*. If not, it should be simple and quite rhythmic: *Prends pitié de nous, Seigneur* (7 syllables – In English, "Have mercy on us, Lord" – 6 syllables). Otherwise, you might use more tune-worthy syllables, paying special attention to the words ending in a silent "e": *Montre-nous ta grâce!* ("Show us your grace!" MNA 41-18).[42]

- The melody consists of an antecedent (the intention) and an answer (the response). The ending of the refrain should not be so conclusive that the cantor cannot easily take up the song. The tradition indicates that the last refrain can have an ending that is melodically conclusive.

The Prayers of the Faithful

Their history

From a pastoral perspective, the restoration by the reform of Vatican II of the prayers of the faithful to the Mass celebrated with a congregation was very important. This rite had disappeared from the Roman liturgy in the sixth century.

---

[40] The presider's greeting should not become a mini-homily on what follows.

[41] MNA 41-16. This book provides other examples of opening litanies for feasts and Sundays of the year.

[42] *Seigneur, prends pitié* ("Lord, have mercy"), the official translation of *Kyrie eleison* in the French Missal, seems very inadequate for singing; its rhythm is out of balance (whereas the inverse, *Prends pitié, Seigneur* ["Have mercy, Lord"], is properly balanced.) It is made up of unvoiced, hard syllables, with no feminine rime to allow it to breathe and make room for neumes. Fortunately, other formulations of the refrain are allowed in the litanic form described above.

The solemn prayers of Good Friday provide a venerable witness to this type of prayer that was common to the Christian assembly from its very beginnings. Each petition has three parts: 1) the deacon proclaims the intention; 2) a period of silent prayer; and 3) a concluding presidential prayer, followed by the Amen of the assembly. It is thought that these proclamations date from the church of the martyrs.

The litany of Pope Gelasius (492-496) provides us with the prototype of the genre. We are familiar with its structure: the intention is announced by the deacon or a cantor or reader, followed by an invocation by the assembly: "Lord, hear us and have mercy." In the early days of the renewal in the 1950s, a French version of the Gelasian litany appeared, chanted on a tone inspired by the Roman preface tone, with the refrain, "O Lord, hear and have mercy."[43]

Even when translated into French, Gelasius' prayer is very beautiful; its intentions include all the needs of the church and the world. I wish we heard it more often.

Today

People have welcomed the restored prayer of the faithful. It seems to be used regularly and fairly well. Those who lead liturgies and prepare the intentions take interest in it. Most often the intentions relate to the readings from scripture, to world events and to the gathered assembly. Generally, they are written to be read, rarely to be chanted. The people's response is frequently sung. A fairly large number of generally well-suited refrains has been created for singing.

We still need to find a balance in the movement between the intention and the refrain. Often the intention is too long; sometimes the refrain is also, particularly when it is taken from a song. Then the whole thing gets heavy. If there are too many things in the intention, people no longer know what they are praying for when they get to the refrain. The length of the intention and of the refrain should be proportional, so that the rhythm of the whole prayer unfolds harmoniously.

It does not seem appropriate to always accompany the intentions, but harmony can make the refrain more powerful.

Normally there should be a brief time for silent prayer after the prayer intention has been announced. Unfortunately, this is rarely observed. Actually, it poses a practical "how-to" problem: if we stop after the intention, how does everyone begin the refrain together after the silence? The best solution is to have the cantor

---

[43] It appeared in *Musique et Liturgie,* 1953 (Fiche B 19). A more ornate version was published in *150 chants* by CNPL in 1984. The text can be found in *Prière du temps présent,* morning and evening prayer of Thursday of the Fourth Week.

end the silence with an *ekphonesis*,* which gives the signal for the assembly to respond by singing, for example, "Together, let us pray." Note, in this case, that the end of the cantor's phrase should prepare a natural reprise of the refrain.

The "Lamb of God" and the Song for the Fraction Rite

The current litany

The *Agnus Dei* is the shortest of all the litanies. The invocation uses John the Baptist's words to point out the Messiah: "Behold the Lamb of God who takes away the sins of the world." But it also hints at Isaiah's description of the lamb being led to the slaughter. The two sides of the paschal mystery are represented, the passion of the sacrificial Lamb and the risen Lamb. This invocation is repeated three times.

Its supplication is the most common: "Have mercy on us." But the last time, we respond, "Grant us peace," no doubt because it is so close to the exchange of peace.

The GIRM provides for repeating the invocation as often as necessary to accompany the action of the breaking of bread (56c).

The introduction of the Lamb of God in Rome is attributed to Pope Sergius I in the seventh century. But most other liturgies, in Milan, Gaul, and Spain, already had special chants for the rites of sharing the bread. In addition, in Rome the fraction accompanied secondary rites that were fairly complex and needed time. Our Lamb of God may be a substitute for, or an abbreviated version of, a more developed earlier chant.

In its current state, the Lamb of God presents no special problem. Whether the song moves back and forth between cantor and congregation on each invocation and response, or all sing from beginning to end, its performance flows easily.

Among the many settings of the official French text of the ordinary of the Mass, the Lamb of God has often been the most successful piece. Thus we have at our disposal a significant repertoire of very usable music.

A song for the sharing of bread?

Today the question posed by the song for the sharing of bread[44] is not musical, but sacramental and ritual.

---

* *Ekphonesis*: a bridge (lead-in) between spoken or silent prayer and song. – Translator

[44] I have deliberately chosen to speak of "sharing" rather than of "breaking." This latter word evokes above all the aspects of breaking and tearing. The word "sharing" brings out better the positive aspect of the supper of the Lord who gives himself to all, and still evokes his gift of love in his body given up for us.

Among the Lord's foundational gestures at the last supper (taking bread, blessing it, sharing and giving it), the sharing of bread seems to have most deeply left its mark on the disciples.[45] We can even say that it was the first name for the Mass. It remains its most eloquent gesture.

As the rite is currently celebrated, this foundational gesture seems to be obliterated by an accumulation of texts and rites, in particular by the exchange of peace that immediately precedes it.

The presider and the ministers distribute a piece of this one bread to everyone.[46]

Today I would like to see this gesture of sharing developed further.

If this rite were longer and more visible, it would be an occasion for a more highly developed song that could voice some of the unfathomable aspects of the mystery of sharing. The Milanese rite already uses a chant with a variable text for this purpose. For participants in the Lord's supper who are preparing for communion, this is an appropriate time for a sung meditation.

Possible forms

Several forms would suit this song of sharing:

- additional invocations for the Lamb of God as were done in the ninth and tenth centuries. Examples of this are available in several already published songs.[47]

- a verbo-melodic antiphon, possibly based on a scriptural text, with verses in trope style.

- a simple, meditative strophic song that would invite everyone to meditate on the mystery of sharing.[48]

Such a song could imbue this essential gesture of the Lord's supper with meaning and depth, and enable all those who have heard, "Take and eat...Take and drink" to better prepare for the peak sacramental moment of communion.

---

[45] Think of the disciples of Emmaus who recognized the Lord in this gesture (Luke 24.30) or Paul's catechesis on it in 1 Corinthians 10:16-19.

[46] See *Dans vos assemblées*, pp. 481-484, where the question is asked and developed. The kiss of peace can be returned to its original place, which is, as in other rites, before the eucharistic prayer.

[47] For example, *Voici l'Agneau de Dieu* ("Behold the Lamb of God") with verses for different liturgical seasons (AL 200 – MNA 28.20); also *Tu as ouvert le livre* ("You have opened the book" AL 179-MNA 28-29); also based on a venerable text is *De la table du Seigneur* ("From the table of the Lord" D 80-MNA 29-23).

Many English Mass settings have these alternate invocations; for example Mass of Glory by Bob Hurd and Marty Haugen's Mass of Creation. – Editor

[48] For example, *Pain que l'on partage* ("Bread that we share" D21-86) or *Un peu de pain que l'on partage* ("This morsel of bread that we share" D 200-MNA 29-29).

In English, examples of this type of song include Christopher Willcock's "This Body" or the Taizé composition "Eat This Bread" – Editor

Chapter 6

THE EUCHARISTIC PRAYER

At the summit of the Mass stands the eucharistic prayer, the hymn of praise and thanksgiving of the Christian paschal feast. Since the reform of Vatican II, we can hear and understand the words of this great table blessing of those whom the Lord has invited to share his banquet.

But can we easily recognize the meaning of this prayer, which "the entire congregation joins itself to Christ in acknowledging the great things God has done and in offering the sacrifice" (GIRM 54)? Too often the eucharistic prayer is experienced as a long monologue. The priest reads from a book, interrupted a first time by the singing of the Sanctus and a second time by the memorial acclamation. If we look at the history of the sung Mass, we might ask if we have not taken a step backwards in relation to the former state where everything was "music": the preface was sung, the first part of the *Sanctus* was sung, bells rang during the consecration and then the *Benedictus* and the "*Per omnia*...Amen." Certainly the whole assembly needed to hear the "wondrous deeds of the God" to be able to give thanks for them, but the eucharistic prayer, as it is too often presented, seems to be chopped up and unmusical.

Yet the dynamic of the torrent of words that carries us forward speaks as much as the content of the words. The structure of the prayer, which we already find in the three Jewish table blessings, uses in succession:

1. Praise to the Creator for his wonders, which moves into the Seraphic hymn, the Holy, Holy.

2. Thanksgiving for all of God's actions in the history of salvation, climaxing in the memorial of the death and resurrection of the Lord.

3. Petitions that what is proclaimed be accomplished and that the new world come.

The whole is crowned by a final doxology and the Amen of the whole assembly. Both the elements of each part and the assembly's interventions are carefully articulated among themselves. In the diagram on the facing page I attempt to show how this holds together.

INITIAL DIALOGUE AND PREFACE

As we have already noted, first the one who serves as presider in the name of the Lord present among the people united in his name asks the assembly their assent for him to exercise his ministry.

Only in the case of the eucharistic prayer does the initial dialogue develop as if, in order to raise us to the heights in common praise, the presider needs more momentum. The tone rises three times, as on eagles' wings: each time all affirm it. "It is right to give him thanks and praise," says the assembly. The presider takes it up in the name of all present: "We do well always and everywhere to give you thanks...."

The traditional chanting tones given for this dialogue in the French Missal match the words well. The whole dialogue presupposes and calls for a lively, resonant, unified outpouring.

The link between the dialogue and the preface happens naturally. We have already addressed the question of chanting the prefaces (p. 136). Within the Mass, the end of the preface features a melodic turn that remains suspended (on the sub-tonic) in a way as to call forth the Holy, Holy and—if possible—links it directly to the Holy, Holy without any break, change of key or introduction.

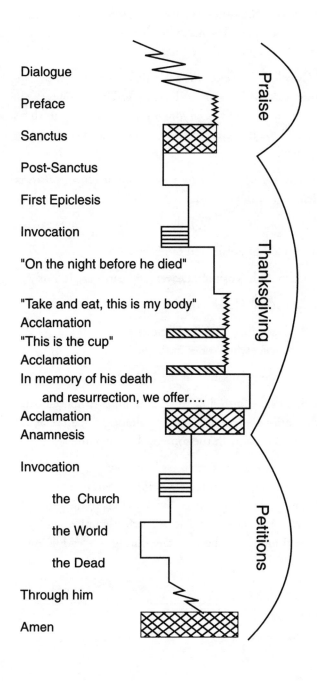

Dialogue

Preface

Sanctus

Post-Sanctus

First Epiclesis

Invocation

"On the night before he died"

"Take and eat, this is my body"
Acclamation
"This is the cup"
Acclamation
In memory of his death
    and resurrection, we offer....
Acclamation
Anamnesis

Invocation

the Church

the World

the Dead

Through him

Amen

Praise

Thanksgiving

Petitions

THE SERAPHIC HYMN (THE HOLY, HOLY)

The outline that the third-century *Apostolic Tradition* furnishes to those who lead the eucharistic prayer has no indication of responses from the assembly between the initial dialogue and the final Amen.

"Holy! Holy!" This evokes the song that Isaiah heard the angels calling out to one another during his vision in the temple. Their song is the heavenly pattern of our earthly songs; it draws everyone into participating in this seraphic hymn. Little by little, all the liturgies have adopted it as part of the praise section of the eucharistic prayer.

In its current form, the *Sanctus* is not a homogeneous text, but a patchwork of several elements of biblical origin:

(A) Adoration: Holy, holy, holy

(B) Lord, God of power and might,

(C) Proclamation (cosmic): heaven and earth are full of your glory.

(B') Acclamation: Hosanna in the highest.

(C') 2nd proclamation (christological):
Blessed is he who comes in the name…

(B") Acclamation: Hosanna in the highest.

Each element calls forth different and complementary attitudes from the assembly: adoration, wonder, exclamation, blessing, final exclamation; the assembly unites itself invisibly with the song of the seraphim.

Can the song express such richness in its own way? The *Sanctus XVIII* of the Gregorian *Kyriale* is a point of reference for the vocal expression of the words of this hymn. This piece has been saved for us thanks to the liturgy for the dead. We know its age from the way the melody is perfectly linked with the preface chant, which is in the B mode that became rare during the Middle Ages.

di - cén - tes :   Sanc - tus

What the musical composition of this piece teaches us is very illuminating:

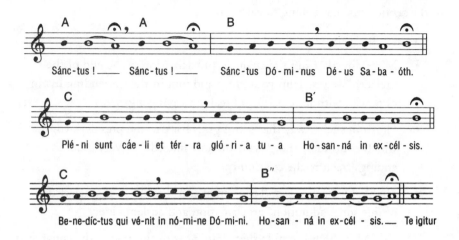

The repetition of the same melody on the two first words, "Holy! Holy!" clearly suggests the alternating song of the Seraphim, "who call to each other, 'Holy, Holy'" (Isaiah 6:2-3) in a posture of adoration. The names of God that follow are proclaimed on the chanting tone, which gives them great strength.

The first proclamation (C) and the second (C') likewise use the chanting tone B, with the preparation tones (G-A), the mediant cadence A, the verbal accent C, and the final cadence (A-G).

The first acclamation (B') after the intonation finishes with a feminine cadence that returns to the dominant B. But the last acclamation (B"), despite the identical text, does not use the same melody. It actually prepares a suspended cadence on the sub-tonic A to lead the presider's chant to the B. Unfortunately this sub-tonic cadence is no longer heard as such today; it seems to be an ending in A minor, while we ought to hear it as a suspension that prepares for what follows.

Analyzing this model helps us better understand what sort of musical treatment the text of the Sanctus calls for. The majority of settings of this text have used classical forms of the assembly's song, which, however, do not move well enough from the preface to the prayer that follows.

For example, let's look at the responsorial form that uses "Hosanna in the highest!" as its refrain. This refrain neutralizes the attitudes envisaged by the different phrases of the song. It becomes a closed, self-sufficient piece of music.

In a different vein, the chorale form, in which the text is treated as a stanza of a hymn whose melody moves with its own logic, cannot express the meaning or the sentiments that belong to each phrase.

To sum up, this music should:

- Move directly from the chant or proclamation at the end of the preface, "we proclaim your glory and join in their unending hymn of praise" without creating a break or leaving a gap.

- Finish in such a way that it brings us back to the presider's voice, which continues, "Lord, you are holy indeed...." Very loud endings fracture the continuity.

- Highlight the words and the verbal acts that are so characteristic of this song: adoration, proclamation and acclamation.

The GIRM is careful to note that "joining with the angels, the congregation sings or recites the Sanctus" (55b). This assumes that:

- The music is rhythmically and melodically accessible to all congregations, without being banal or needing accompaniment.

- Its admissibility and ability to withstand repeated use are proven.

A polyphonic setting and instruments are not excluded insofar as they fulfill the ritual demands indicated above.

The Memorial Acclamation

The only acclamation sung by the assembly in the Roman canon was the Sanctus. In the eucharistic prayers of the Eastern liturgies, however, the assembly participates through a variety of acclamations, litanies and tropes.

The restoration of the eucharistic prayer said aloud in the vernacular gave rise to the wish that the congregation actively associate itself to the greatest praise of the people whom God has saved.

Thus the reform of the Mass allowed the people to sing the acclamation called the anamnesis because it is in remembering the Lord's death and resurrection that his self-offering is realized in the eucharistic meal. As Paul said in his first letter to the Corinthians (11:26), "Every time you eat this bread and drink this cup, you proclaim the death of the Lord until he comes."

The French Missal gives three formulas for the text and music of this acclamation. They are currently in use. Several other existing texts allow more typical musical settings. In general, it is a positive and successful element of the liturgical reform.

Where Does This Acclamation Belong?

The prayer of thanksgiving in which the institution narrative finds its place culminates in the presidential prayer that follows the institution narrative: "In memory of his death and resurrection, we offer you, Father...." Originally the plan had been to conclude this prayer with an acclamation of praise like those commonly found in the eastern rites. Only the memorial acclamation was kept, introduced by the words, "Let us proclaim the mystery of faith."

The expression "mystery of faith" had been removed from the words of consecration of the cup since they were not part of the authentic words of consecration, but Pope Paul VI wanted to keep the expression, therefore, it was proposed as the *ekphonesis*[49] to introduce the memorial acclamation. That is how this new acclamation came to be inserted between the institution narrative and the memorial prayer.

When using this acclamation, you will notice the anomaly of putting the assembly's anamnesis before the presider's, which cuts off the latter from the narrative to which it belongs. This is why the congregation's acclamation follows the priest's prayer in the eucharistic prayers for Masses with children written some years later; it thus concludes the thanksgiving section of the eucharistic prayer.

The Usefulness of the *Ekphonesis*

When the celebrant (or when he cannot, a cantor) proclaims in song, "Let us proclaim the mystery of faith," the assembly immediately sings, "Christ has died...."

If this introduction to the memorial acclamation is missing, whatever precedes the acclamation must create this linkage. It's very bad when one voice begins and the congregation joins in bit by bit. An organ introduction is out of place at this point. When the memorial acclamation follows the memorial prayer, as we have said, it is normal that this prayer would be chanted as the climax of our thanksgiving. It can then be concluded in a manner that allows the acclamation to emerge from it.

---

[49] Recall that *ekphonesis* is a Greek word that means "a voice outside." It designates the very widespread procedure in the Eastern liturgies in which the priest intones a few words that lead back into song after prayers have been said quietly. The priest used to do this in Latin at the end of the secret or the canon when he intoned *"per omnia saecula saeculorum"* so that the congregation could sing "Amen."

A Prayer Addressed to Christ

Some people are astonished that the acclamation is addressed to Christ: "*Nous rappelons ta mort*" ("Remembering your death" = "Dying you destroyed our death") in the middle of a prayer entirely addressed to the Father. Is this logical?

In fact, this corresponds to the quasi-original usage of Christian prayer. The presider prays to the Father in the name of the whole assembly, but the faithful pray to the One who leads us to the Father.

OTHER ACCLAMATIONS

Thanksgiving

As I mentioned, the most common acclamation in the Eastern-rite anaphora is the formula of praise and thanksgiving:

We sing your praises,

We bless you,

We give you thanks,

And we pray to you, our Father.

The reform anticipated this. Rather than impose it, it left the door open for the possibility of using it. This was the case with the eucharistic prayers for Masses with children. Here it is in an elementary form:

We praise you! We bless you! We thank you!

I hope that creative inculturation will be inspired by these examples to highlight the assembly's participation when that seems desirable.

The Invocations of the Holy Spirit

A good example of this kind of inculturation in French-speaking countries is found in the epicleses that prolong the two prayers that are situated before the institution narrative (epiclesis of consecration) and after the memorial prayer, at the beginning of the petition section (epiclesis of communion).

For example, for the first epiclesis:

May the Spirit of God most holy come to

Sanctify for us this bread and this cup.

And for the second:

> May the Spirit of God most holy come to
>
> Gather us into a single body![50]

Each one of these invocations needs to be introduced by an *ekphonesis*.

THE FINAL DOXOLOGY

All the new eucharistic prayers conclude with the doxology borrowed from the Roman canon: "Through him, with him and in him…." to which the whole assembly responds "Amen."

If possible, the presider, and possibly concelebrants, should chant this doxology, using the tone provided in the Sacramentary.

How can the assembly's final Amen have the fullness needed to capture the solemn conclusion of all this eucharistic praise?

- The Amen can be extended by a melisma, which gives a beautiful effect, but this solution will not work with every congregation.

- Another frequently used solution is to repeat the amen several times; each time is louder or the pitch is raised by a tone. Harmony may be added. These solutions are not always convincing; sometimes they seem contrived. People can tire of them.

You might explore some of the possibilities in the eucharistic prayers for children. For example, in the French translation of Eucharistic Prayer II for Masses with Children, we read:

With him, we sing your praise,

With him, we bless you,

Glory to you, our Father

Now and for ever

Amen! Amen!

This text paves the way for solidly constructed music that all congregations can sing. Other similar formulas have met with a certain success.

---

[50] Other examples are found in MNA 26.71 and following.

When presiders take advantage of the variety of chanting or speaking tones in the presidential prayers, and the assembly participates in acclamations that express the meaning and structure of the eucharistic prayer, the eucharistic prayer offers an image of this highest form of praise rising to the Lord from the people he has saved.

CHAPTER 7

HYMNS AND SPIRITUAL SONGS

A HISTORY

The church was born singing. After singing the Hallel psalms (Matthew 26:30), Jesus left the upper room to embark on the journey that would renew all creation.

While they were in prison at Philippi, Paul and Silas sang God's praises in the middle of the night, to the astonishment of the other prisoners (Acts of the Apostles 16:25). The letter to the Colossians exhorts the Christians of that community to sing hymns, psalms and spiritual songs in their assemblies; to sing every kind of song, provided that it is done in the Spirit and in a spirit of thanksgiving (Colossians 3:16).

Pliny the Younger described the behavior of Christians to the Emperor Trajan around the year 115; typically, they assembled at an appointed time before dawn to sing hymns to one *Chrêstos*, as to a god (Ep. 10.96.7).

By the third century, the production of Christian hymns was widespread and abundant. Eusebius of Caesarea spoke of Nepos, the author of many hymns that enjoyed much success among fellow believers (*Ecclesiastical History* 7, 14, 4). On the other hand, song was also the heretics' great weapon for spreading their doctrine.

What was this hymnody like?

If we go back to the very first generations of Christians, we find the Odes of Solomon, which indicate the heights of poetic lyricism already attained by Christian literature:

As the occupation of the ploughsman is ploughing,

And the occupation of the helmsman is the steering of the ship,

So also my occupation is the palm of the Lord by his hymns.[51]

However, we do not know how widely read or used these creations were.

On the other hand, liturgical tradition has maintained two witnesses to ancient hymnody whose roots are in the second century: the "Glory to God" which the Roman Mass adopted from the Byzantine office of matins, and the evening hymn, also from the Eastern liturgies, which the reform of Vatican II returned to the Liturgy of the Hours:

Joyous light,

Eternal splendor of the Father

Holy and blessed Jesus Christ.

It is remarkable that this hymn writing does not come out of the Greek or Latin classical poets, but from a kind of rhythmic prose. What is said in sung words has won out over the devices of poetry.

Earlier (p. 102), I described the Latin strophic hymnody of Ambrose of Milan at the end of the fourth century. It gave birth to countless descendants from the Middle Ages right down to our own time. We also mentioned the role of the sequence and the thousands of creations that stemmed from it over the centuries, as well as the great variety of popular songs in the vernacular, especially since the Reformation (pp. 103-104). The creation of Christian hymns is an uninterrupted phenomenon. What is its place today in the Mass of the Roman Rite?

IN THE MASS

It may appear astonishing to argue that, alone among all the liturgical rites, the Roman rite did not welcome strophic hymns into its liturgy. In the West, the hymns of St. Ambrose found their way quickly enough into the monastic office, and later into the Roman office, but never into the Mass.

---

[51] *The Odes of Solomon*, edited and translated by James H. Charlesworth (Missoula, MT: Scholars Press, 1977), Ode 16, p. 70.

We must nevertheless mention two special cases: the Glory to God in lyrical prose and, from the Middle Ages, the sequences after the Alleluia with their own rhythms.

To enrich the song of the assembly, the reform of Vatican II opened the doors to hymns as a song of thanksgiving after communion:

"If desired, a hymn, psalm or other song of praise may be sung by the entire congregation (GIRM 56j)."

In fact, along with the Glory to God, this is the only song that in and of itself is an autonomous rite for the whole assembly. It is because of this that we deal with hymns here under four forms:

• ancient hymnody: the Glory to God;

• the song accompanying the Word of God:
   sequences and similar pieces;

• strophic hymns (the post-communion song); and

• songs with refrains (various uses).

The Glory to God

In the unfolding of the Mass, the Glory to God is a festive song. It was introduced into the Roman Mass in the sixth century for the feast of Christmas, after which its use was extended to other feasts, and eventually to Sundays outside of Advent and Lent.

Its structure

The lyrical prose hymn is a treasure of Christian prayer. Rooted in the earliest centuries of the church, it brings together in a very clear structure a series of elements that have evolved.

The opening acclamation is that of the angels on Christmas night (Luke 1:14).
   Glory to God in the highest heaven,*
   and peace on earth to those whom he loves![52]

---

* In order to follow Gelineau's line of thought, the text here is a more literal translation of the French version of the Glory to God rather than the current English liturgical text. – *Editor*

[52] Luke's original text reads "and on the earth peace for men of good will [of God]." Because of the Latin *bonae voluntatis,* this expression was long translated as "and peace to men of good will." To eliminate this contradiction, the French liturgical text reads "And peace to people whom he loves." But this translation is doubly regrettable, first because *qui l'aime* ("whom he loves") and *qui l'aiment* ("whom they love") sound the same in French. Who loves whom? But there is a second issue, the question that is often raised: "And the others? Those God doesn't love?" A clear translation would be, "Peace to people, for God loves them."

A first strophe addresses God the Father:

> We praise you, we bless you we adore you,
>
> We glorify you, we give you thanks for your great glory.
>
> Lord God, King of heaven, God the Father all-powerful

A second strophe is addressed to Christ. After proclaiming his principal titles:

> Lord, only Son, Jesus Christ,
>
> Lord God, Lamb of God, Son of the Father

It petitions him three times:

> you take away the sin of the world: have mercy on us;
>
> you take away the sin of the world: receive our prayer;
>
> you are seated at the right hand of the Father: have mercy on us.

The third strophe takes up the initial praise, but this time addresses it to the Son. It concludes with the Trinitarian formula: "For you alone are Holy, you alone are Lord, you alone are the Most High, Jesus Christ, with the Holy Spirit, in the glory of God the Father."

Sung-through or alternating?

The angelic hymn has been sung in different ways throughout the centuries. Undoubtedly the Glory to God began as an uninterrupted chant using a melodic formula that was repeated from phrase to phrase. The Ambrosian Gloria has furnished us with a very beautiful example, rooted in the B mode of the Mediterranean basin. It is in number XV of the Roman *Kyriale*.

Gregorian chant most often used verbo-melodism in setting the Gloria. Different settings are more or less rich, but they always stick to the words of the hymn. The song is conceived to be sung by two alternating choirs.

Other settings such as the Gloria of the Mass of the Angels reflect the tastes of different eras. The end of the seventeenth century saw the flowering of plainchant, particularly in the Masses of Du Mont. Parish congregations can sing this style of chant.

Because the Gloria always was a major component of the sung Masses, we have many arrangements and concert settings based on the Latin text.

What is the situation today?

Since the vernacular languages were introduced into the liturgy, dozens of French settings of the new official text have appeared. In these, the Glory to God has been set either in free rhythm or in a measured melody that remains more or less true to the text. Some settings pay attention to the structure of the text; others do not.

Unfortunately, few parishes have made the effort to learn a sung-through setting of the Glory to God.

More recently, several settings have appeared that reflect the structure of the text. It is too soon to assess how well these different creations that have been used by only a very few parishes will be received.

On one hand, I regret that parishes are now missing out on the grace that belongs to a song that for a long time was sung by heart from one end to the other. This was a unique time of lyrical prayer during the Mass. On the other hand, I recognize that except for the high feast days, three songs for a single entrance rite constitute ritual overload. Simply reciting the Glory to God does not really do justice to this prayer that is meant to be sung. No doubt it would be better to save it for the festive days for which it had been originally introduced into the Roman Mass.

In responsorial form

Since most parishes turned their backs on sung-through settings of the Glory to God, several other settings have been proposed. First, there was the responsorial form, which consisted of a short refrain with verses sung by a soloist.

While I will not deny the practical interest of this type of easy arrangement for the assembly, it is worth noting that the responsorial form is already frequently used during the Mass. This form breaks up the lyrical flow of the original hymn; it can quickly become tedious and wearisome.

In strophic form

The body of the hymn is treated as two equal strophes. The first is addressed to the Father. The second is addressed to the Son and concludes with the Trinitarian confession. Naturally enough, the initial acclamation serves as a refrain (for example, F 156).

The popularity of this form is undeniable and in German-speaking countries it is seen as fully liturgical. It is worth noting that in this strophic form the Glory to God makes a very good entrance song for ordinary Sundays, especially during the Christmas season. But despite its clear pastoral appeal, this genre cannot replace verbo-melodism based on the original text.

THE MEDITATION SONG

Sources

I have alluded to the important body of liturgical songs based on prose and sequences that was created during the Middle Ages. We saw that these lyrical works were inserted after the alleluia, between the epistle and the gospel. The Lutheran cantata would eventually flower here. Thus these pieces are linked to the biblical word and, on feast days, to the mystery highlighted that day.

Now, I would suggest that since we have been using the Missal of Paul VI, a certain lyrical frustration with the Liturgy of the Word is becoming more and more evident. In the thirty minutes or so that the Liturgy of the Word lasts, song is often limited to the psalm refrain, the gospel acclamation (and often the accompanying verses are not sung), and the response of the prayers of the faithful, if it is sung at all. These are nothing but scraps. Such celebrations lack the opportunities to breathe that real song provides, what we experienced in the sung high Mass and can still see in the Eastern rites.

This situation explains in part the initiatives and research undertaken on the possibility of having a "meditation song" that would enable the assembly to appropriate and deepen the biblical message of the day.

Place

It seems that the best place in the liturgy for this would be after the silence after the homily and before the prayers of the faithful.

Already some songs pick up on gospel narratives such as the disciples on the road to Emmaus, or the appearance of Jesus at the lakeside, and above all, the great gospels of the scrutinies that come up during the readings of Lent, Year A: the Samaritan woman, the man born blind, the raising up of Lazarus. Different pieces have been written to help people make a deeper connection between their own lives and the gospel message, especially in parishes where there are catechumens.

The inevitable objection to this is: "It's going to make a Mass that's already overloaded even longer."

Healthy pastoral liturgical practice always knows how to determine what is good and fruitful for this assembly; how long the opening rites should be, the optimal number of scriptural readings, and the length of the homily, which listeners often find too long. We must find the best way of nurturing the word that has been planted within us. As I said earlier, we must work pastorally to make our Liturgies of the Word less intellectualized, particularly since people are less familiar with them, by finding a new balance between word and song.

Forms

Because song enables the assembly to ponder, meditate on and repeat the word, and because the assembly gives praise and thanks for the message it has received, it is essential that the assembly itself be the first agent of this part of the celebration. A song with a refrain would be frustrating and less fruitful because the very people who are ruminating on the word are not singing the verses. The strophic hymn in which everyone sings all the strophes would allow everyone to appropriate the message more readily. Yet the strophic hymn risks seeming to be too static and too compact. To meditate on the word, we need to be able to breathe; we need to introduce some contrasting, alternating elements.

A certain number of songs that already exist lend themselves to these dialogue structures and are within the reach of many congregations.[53]

Here we should take another look at the sequence[54] or similar models. Remember that the sequence is sung by two choirs. The second choir, which might be the congregation responding to a cantor, takes up the melody it just heard, but uses different words. This allows the congregation to take up the word again in a way that moves through the message that has been proclaimed. After each pair, the melody changes, moving the story forward.

In this way the word, which was first proclaimed in the reading and then explained in the homily, is repeated and pondered. This process sheds light on the word and makes it more appealing.

THE HYMN AFTER COMMUNION

As I noted earlier, one of the innovations of Vatican II was that it made room in the Mass for a thanksgiving hymn after communion if the community so desired (GIRM 56h).

---

[53] For example: *Que cherchez-vous au soir tombant?* ("What are you looking for as evening falls?" I78); *Qui donc est là sur le rivage?* ("Say, who is on the shore?" MNA35-83); etc. Another very precious resource for internalizing the word is the *Cantilénes bibliques*, Éd. Studio SM.

[54] After the Council of Trent, the reform of Pius V kept only four sequences in the Roman Missal: *Victimae paschali*, *Lauda sion*, *Stabat Mater*, etc.) They are scarcely usable except in Latin and are optional in the Missal of Paul VI. However, the sequence for Easter has inspired a few good songs in French, such as *Sans avoir vu nous le croyons* ("Without seeing, we believe" I 168).

Forms

The form is to be: "A hymn, psalm or another song of praise" according to the General Instruction.

You could use one of the alleluiatic psalms, such as Psalm 116 (MNA29.51) or Psalm 112 (MNA 29.52). Another good possibility would be a responsorial song of praise, such as the prayer of the *Didache*, "Our Father, we give you thanks … glory to you for the ages." These lively forms presuppose a fairly homogeneous congregation that participates well. This produces a very beautiful period of thanksgiving.

The Strophic Hymn

The strophic hymn offers a richer and more varied repertoire. Since Vatican II, a great number of hymns of real merit have been written in French. Many were written for the Liturgy of the Hours, and dealt with the mysteries of Christ throughout the liturgical seasons. These creations are still rarely used in parishes. However, a number of them would work very well as the hymn after communion, for example, *Dieu est à l'oeuvre en cet âge* ("God is at work in these times" MNA46-16).*

Turning to the strophic form for this ritual moment is easily justified: singing the hymn is itself the ritual act. We are doing nothing else but praising and thanking God together. This form calls for the assembly's ongoing, single-hearted participation through all the verses. It is a peak moment that expresses the communion of all just before the assembly scatters once more.

This type of musical moment is unique in the Mass.

CANTICLES WITH REFRAINS

Unless it designates a biblical poem that is not part of the Book of Psalms (for example, the canticle of Mary), the word "canticle" has no precise musicological meaning. Most frequently it is applied to a religious song in the vernacular. Our Protestant brothers and sisters use the words *psalms* and *canticles* for two categories of songs used in worship. In Western Catholicism, any song that is not in Latin can be called a canticle. In the vernacular languages used in the Roman liturgy, the word can be applied to ritual songs. Thus it can be applied to pieces of many forms in the Mass.

---

* English songs of praise abounds in every style from "Holy God, We Praise Thy Name," Clarence Walworth's translation of *Grosser Gott,* itself a version of the *Te Deum,* also the source of Christopher Idle's "God We Praise You," to Jan Vermulst's version of Psalm 150 to Dan Schutte's "Sing a New Song" and Christopher Walker's "Sing of the Lord's Goodness." – Editor

Included with canticles we thus can find strophic hymns, songs with refrains, and litanies. Their texts can be taken from or inspired by scripture, liturgical rites, individual meditations, or simple devotions.

In each case therefore we should examine a canticle's text and music to determine its form and to see if the whole piece can fit a particular ritual moment of the Mass.

Fortunately, it seems that most canticles written since the liturgical renewal of the 1940s have been based on the Bible or the liturgy and are designed for ritual use, for feasts or liturgical seasons, for predetermined times in the Mass, and so on. But the ritual use of some is not clear.

Ritual Functions

Normally we would not substitute canticles for fixed ritual songs that have canonical texts we are obliged to use, such as acclamations, the songs of the ordinary[55] of the Mass, the Lord's Prayer, and so on.

They would be principally used as processionals: at the entrance, the preparation of the gifts and Communion. Since canticles often have a refrain, alternating between the verses and the refrain works well when people are moving.

But if the piece is written in pure strophic form, canticles can also be used when people are not moving, such as for the hymn after communion. If the canticle has an alternating form, it could be used for the meditation song.

Fortunately, most French texts available to us were created expressly for the liturgy in the vernacular and for the actual rites of the Mass. In these cases, they are more and more rarely called canticles, and are more frequently designated by their form: hymn, *troparion*, litany, processional, antiphon, response, and so on.

But we would not have been able to create this repertoire if we had not had at our disposal, in addition to contemporary compositions, a treasury of popular religious melodies (old noëls, Breton airs, etc.) to which contemporary words can be perfectly fit.

---

[55] Some legitimate variations can exist, especially in two instances foreseen by the Roman instruction on liturgical translations (LMD 98): When there exists in the song a text that has been received before the canonical text; when the official text creates difficulties for producing good music (36d).

Chapter 8

IN TUNE, IN TIME:
ACCURACY AND PACING

"Accuracy" and "pacing" are two familiar expressions to musicians. The correct pitch and appropriate tempo are two essential qualities for all music.

These qualities are also essential for liturgy. Ritual, like music, is an art. Anything destined to become symbol and sacrament (gesture, word, objects, space) must be just what is necessary. It cannot be too little or too much.

This kind of *justice* in our ritual behaviors is rooted in the same word and the same vision as biblical justice:* the manifestation and realization here and now of God's action that creates the world anew.

Clarifying what this means for the practice of liturgical song does not take us away from our task at hand. But first a few remarks are necessary.

Good tone and correct pitch are relative terms.

Absolute pitch does not exist. It is always relative to culture and cultural situations. The ear hears the same intervals as on pitch or off pitch depending on musical traditions, the instruments used, the influences of other cultures, the nature of the climate, and so on. We know that in our tempered scale, every interval except the octave is out of tune in relationship to natural harmonics. Nonetheless, today we measure the accuracy of our ear by them.

In similar fashion, the way people measure the right pitch for sacred song is not the same for Africans, who dance as they sing, as it is for Northern Europeans, who sing a chorale as they sit in their pew. Likewise, the expected and

---

*The author plays on the two French words, *justesse* (accuracy) and *justice* (justice), which can be traced back to the Latin words *iustus/iustitia*: justice/what is right. – Translator

accepted style we use for Christmas varies significantly from what we use on an ordinary Sunday. Nor do we use the same criteria for an assembly made up of elders as for one composed of young people.

We can also expect that there will be significant differences between the judgment of a professional musician and that of the person on the street. This does not mean that one is necessarily right and the other wrong. In most popular folklore, *portamento* is used; the pitch of the singer's voice can float, notes quaver; different attacks are used, each variation having its own expressive value. Gregorian chant no doubt used these vocal techniques. In some of the Eastern churches, their cantors must use a strong nasal voice that we find shocking.

I would like to make some general observations about what might be accepted as a good style of celebrating in today's French liturgical assemblies.

ONLY ONE STYLE OF SINGING

When we like one style of singing, it is a temptation to use only songs in that particular style: only canticles with a refrain, only chorales, only *faux-bourdons*, only rhythmic music, only music in harmony, only whichever style.

Everything I have said in this book about the riches of the various forms of vocal expression found in the liturgy shows well enough that the celebration will be impoverished if it is deprived of the various forms of song that belong to it.

Note that I have not said, "Nothing but Gregorian," because Gregorian chant, understood in the broadest sense, has preserved all the forms of Christian ritual song, even though the uniform way of singing it does not always let us see that.

TOO MANY OR TOO FEW SONGS

I am willing to say that it would not be possible to sing too much in Christian worship; in the great liturgical traditions, everything was or still is sung. But we find a great variety of forms: from recitative to vocalization, from unharmonized melodies to pieces rich in harmonies, from the song of a soloist to that of the assembly.

The excess that I am pointing out here is an imbalance in the choral implementation of the music for a Mass; the assembly feels that it is being choked with too many songs that are always changing, or, on the other hand, that they have nothing to sing because everything is sung by a choir and soloists.

SONGS THAT ARE TOO LONG OR TOO SHORT

What I am talking about here is a particular song that is perceived as out of proportion to its ritual function in the whole of a given liturgy.

Some examples of songs that are too short would include a Lamb of God that doesn't last long enough to highlight the gesture of the sharing of bread, a psalm that is too short to allow the assembly the time it needs to enter into the spirit of the psalm, a song for the presentation of gifts that is finished before the gifts have even arrived at the altar.

On the other hand, sometimes you can hear the voices of the assembly fading away from boredom or fatigue. This can happen during the opening rites when the entrance song goes on while the priest is waiting at the altar, when the communion processional goes on and on and trails off, or when the hymn after communion is one or two verses too long to be beautiful or too short so that it leaves people hungry for more.

All this is clearly relative to a particular assembly and must take into account the style of the whole celebration. It is disappointing when the liturgy feels rushed on a feast day.

TOO SHOWY OR TOO FLAT

This type of problem is especially noticeable when soloists or choirs adopt a showy style of singing, or when they look like they're bored or being punished. In each case, we sense that the assembly's prayer has been sidetracked, for in both cases what is meaningful, rather than leading us to the mystery being celebrated, turns back to itself.

The same thing can happen in an assembly that gets itself artificially excited or, on the other hand, sleeps and drags its feet.

TOO MUCH OR NOT ENOUGH MUSIC

No longer is the question one of knowing if there is enough or too much song in a celebration. Things are more subtle: in a given sung part of the Mass we need to ask if the place allotted to music, whether to soloists, choirs, instruments or the assembly, is correct in relationship to the rite itself.

For example, does the music of the *Sanctus* lead to adoration and mystical praise, or present noisy hosannas that, instead of preparing for what comes next, interrupt the movement of the eucharistic prayer?

To answer this sort of question (which can be asked of any kind of song), it is necessary to refer to the ritual function that is proper to each piece, as I have tried to do in this book.

THE FESTIVE AND THE ORDINARY

The meaning of the word "festive" is clear, but the word "ordinary" used to designate the Sundays of Ordinary Time, or the ordinary of the Mass, is unfortunate. It makes us think of what is routine or repetitive, whereas every celebration, lived in faith, is unique.

However, if we didn't have Ordinary Time, we wouldn't have festive seasons. It goes without saying that some rites and songs belong to certain feasts. They would lose their value if they were used every Sunday. We must resist the temptation to turn each Sunday into a major feast, of bringing out the most magnificent settings and all the best-loved songs for every occasion. People tire of these pieces quickly and the songs themselves wear out.

Even when the content is repeated, appropriateness and singing on key still open us to the Spirit's most lavish feast.

THE WORD ENLIVENED BY THE SPIRIT'S BREATH

In uttering the word, the voice must draw on the song's spirit: a spirit of petition or praise, of prophetic proclamation or introspective listening, of the murmur of a psalm or of a paschal hymn.

There is no hard and fast rule for doing this. We must seize the grace of this day, of this assembly, of this moment, and clothe it in its appropriate musical and vocal form.

Because of this no liturgy is ever reduced to the execution of well-oiled ceremonies that can be utterly boring. And only because of this can we recognize those moments of grace that bring the history of salvation to life, here and now, through signs and symbols, music and song.

CHAPTER 9

SUNDAY CELEBRATIONS OF THE WORD

During the 1970s, certain rural parishes in France that could not celebrate Eucharist each week began the practice of "Sunday Celebrations of the Word." Although the vast majority of Christians in the world (including Catholics) who gather on Sunday do not celebrate Eucharist, this was unusual in one of the oldest countries of Christendom. Today we understand its importance better. We need to speak of it here for two principal reasons.

In this assembly of Christians, not only is the Lord present as he had promised, "when two or three are gathered in my name" (Matthew 18:20), but this assembly also offers an authentic image of the local church as already described in the Acts of the Apostles (2:42-45): they were faithful to coming together in the same place, to listen to the word of the gospel, to strengthen their life in common, and to pool their goods and share them with the poorest. Obviously the peak moment of sharing the eucharistic bread was absent, but the sacrament of the church is already there, visible and at work in its assembled members.

The second reason is conjecture on my part. The diminishing number of Sunday Masses celebrated in rural communities, and even in large urban centers, will rapidly become a far more widespread phenomenon in the coming years. Parish mergers are already being undertaken in many dioceses. However, if it is good to strengthen the ties among those who are responsible in a certain area, it would be disastrous to not support local communities, even small ones. They make the church present to all and form the basis of a new evangelization.[56]

The consequence of this argument is that pastoral liturgical ministry, of which the song of the Christian assembly is a part, cannot limit itself to the Mass.

---

[56] On this subject see Pope John Paul II's encyclical, *Redemptoris Missio*, 51, "Ecclesial Basic Communities as a Force for Evangelization."

It needs to deal with all kinds of gatherings and their celebrations. Given that we can anticipate the importance of Sunday gatherings without Eucharist, we must open up the specifics of this question here.[57]

WHAT MODEL OF CELEBRATION DO WE USE?

When people first began to celebrate without a priest on Sunday, they spontaneously used the outline of the Mass minus the eucharistic prayer. Many, however, retained a communion service. Few risked cutting anything else out of the ordinary pattern of the Mass, except perhaps in the opening rites. The largest piece, therefore, was the Liturgy of the Word. This often resulted in a very austere celebration: many words, few ritual gestures, and a variable number of songs.

Recently, a proposal has been made that these communities use the outline of one of the celebrations of the Liturgy of the Hours. It would consist of praise, psalms, a reading from the scriptures, intercessions and the Lord's Prayer. This model certainly is lighter and breathes better. Its structure is basic, but it was developed specifically for communities that sing the office and for those who are already experienced in communal prayer, the Bible and liturgy.

In our own situation, we must first refer to the local communities that celebrate on Sunday.

WHAT KIND OF ASSEMBLY?

First, we must consider the nature of the gathering. These assemblies no longer consist only of Christians who don't want their faith life to die with the closing of their church, or of specialized groups getting together for prayer, as usually happened when these celebrations first began. Rather, it is a question of calling forth evangelical, missionary clusters of people that welcome not just traditional parishioners, but people of every age and background who are seeking God: catechumens, teenagers, children, those who show up only occasionally, and visitors who join active members of the local community. This needs a more open, more flexible model.

A BASIC MODEL

Missionary-oriented Christian groups use a type of analysis of models that enables us to outline three fundamental periods in any celebration:

* a time of prayer

---

57 From 1979 to 1998, I was pastor of a region where three parishes regularly came together every two weeks.

- a time for the word

- a time of intercession and thanskgiving.

All this is to take place in an atmosphere of hospitality and mutual support.

The time of prayer should be long enough to allow those who are still unfamiliar with this experience to move progressively into praise and adoration. It is not built on multiple formulas, but opens us to the sacred, to contemplation, to encountering God and to the action of the Holy Spirit. Song will play an important role here.

The time for the word should let God's word penetrate the heart and ripen there. A single scripture passage, taken if possible from the daily lectionary, that will be proclaimed, explained, meditated, re-read, or restated in song can already offer substantial nourishment for our faith.

The time of intercession (the prayer of the faithful) and thanksgiving (modeled on the preface) will lead us to the Father.

THE ROLE OF SONG

Prayer time needs songs that last. After a hymn of praise that opens the heart and turns it toward God, we can have a long litany, a time of psalmody that gives enough time for us to savor the spoken word, and a Taizé-style *ostinato*.

During the time for the word, we can give pride of place to the meditation song that I already described (p. 158), which takes up in its own way the message that has been heard and explained.

During the time of praise and intercession, we can chant the intercessions and use refrains that everyone repeats. The Lord's Prayer can be spoken or chanted.

This body of songs would thus offer a genuine lyrical space that is open to possibilities of conversion and welcomes grace.

RITES AND SYMBOLS

Even though these assemblies are deprived of the gestures of the Lord's Supper, they must have rites and symbols that open up the range of signs of the mystery. As it happens, almost all these gestures are connected with songs. For example:

- the entrance hymn in which the assembly praises the
  Lord's name accompanies the procession with the cross.

- an acclamation accompanies the entrance of the lectionary in procession.

Candles, flowers and icons will provide visual support to the songs and prayers, enabling the members of this diverse gathering, wherever they might be in their faith journey, to be more aware of the mystery they are celebrating.

A COMPARISON OF THREE OUTLINES

	Assembly	Liturgy of the Hours	Mass
Opening	Entrance hymn	"O God, come to our assistance"	Entrance hymn
Prayers	Song of praise Psalmody Litany	Hymn Psalmody Verses	Glory to God Psalm [*Kyrie* Litany]
Word of God	Acclamation of the Word Biblical reading	Word of God Silence	Readings Homily

ECUMENICAL GATHERINGS

We must hope for and do everything to hasten the coming of the day when Christians of different rites and denominations will no longer celebrate separately in their own churches, but come together to pray, listen to and respond to the word, offer petitions and thanksgiving, as they await the day when we will all be able to share the bread and cup.

Praying and praising together is the primary and normal way of being united as one church in our one Lord. If we do not agree, our common song will not ring true. Our assembly already points to our expectation of unity in Christ. Our song enables us to live this nascent communion because it is the only tangible reality in which we can join together many different voices in one great unison to glorify God as we prefigure here on earth the song of the elect in glory.

If we do this, our different traditions will enrich each other with their songs and music. In the French-speaking world, we already share a good number of identical melodies that offers us a common heritage. May these songs remind us of our common origin.

I believe that using the treasures of our separated brothers and sisters in our local assemblies opens one path toward the unity we long for.

CHAPTER 10

THE NECESSITY OF INCULTURATION

The liturgical reform desired by Vatican II updated the Roman liturgy according to its own Western tradition and its Latin genius. But the Council Fathers were aware that provisions would have to be made to adapt the liturgy "for different groups, regions and peoples" (CSL 38), and that it would be up to the "competent, territorial ecclesiastical authority" (CSL 39) to assess these adaptations.

Since the Council, much progress has been made on the topic of evangelization and celebration, what we now call "inculturation." We recognize these days that the proclamation of the gospel can touch the depths of human hearts and spirits only in and through each people's own culture. We also recognize that inculturation directly concerns the liturgical prayer of the church and the Christian sacraments that should involve the whole person, body, soul and spirit.

There is no cult (public worship) apart from culture, and all culture has its rituals.

OUR CULTURAL SHIFTS

Despite the work that has been progressing on the relationship between worship and culture, it has had little visible impact on our liturgies. After the Council's openness to the vernacular for biblical readings and prayers, as well as to regional repertoires for songs, it seems that everything related to symbols and ritual behaviors has stayed relatively unchanged. Several observations that touch directly or indirectly on the question of song emerge within the French-speaking Western world.

Although our roots are sunk deep into Latin language and culture, although all the regions of France have been Christianized for more than a thousand years and Christendom has dominated our social structures for centuries, it is clear at the beginning of the twenty-first century that we are far from the religious culture of those years.

Many studies have analyzed the cultural changes that the Western world is experiencing. I will restrict myself here to looking at what has changed and what is changing in the Catholic Sunday Mass.

SMALLER CONGREGATIONS

The first characteristic to note is the significant decrease in the number of people who attend Mass on Sunday. Many parish churches are almost empty. The fact of moving from large gatherings to small ones, from full churches to a few people in a nave that is two-thirds empty, necessarily modifies ritual behaviors and meanings.

We can bemoan this decline, or we can delight that this small group may let each person participate in ways both more communal and more personal, more active and more reflective. A small gathering is not necessarily a barrier to Christian worship.[58] Experience would tend to indicate that basic Christian communities, which lend themselves best to a communal celebration of liturgy — praise, word and Eucharist — are made up of between 30 and 150 people.[59]

We need to examine this change, notably so we can make the best possible use of the church building. We need to pull the assembly together so that the group can both see and hear itself; we need to figure out how processions and the proclamation of the word will work and, of special concern to us here, to consider what will enable people to hear voices and instruments, and to participate easily in the assembly's song.

It will demand a lot of imagination to make the best use of our churches, which are often very beautiful, very sacred, very human, so that we can celebrate well and sing well in them. We will have to dare to try things to see how they work. So-called "good principles" could wind up being disastrous in this context.

---

[58] Some historians estimate that during the first generations of Christianity, local gatherings in private homes averaged about 80 people.

[59] Here I want to remind you of the necessity to distinguish properly among three different types of gatherings that celebrate very differently:

- the small group made up of people who come together because of common interests or for their own celebrations (the type of relationship that motivates participation is more important here than the number of participants);

- in contrast, large festive gatherings (pilgrimages, special occasions, etc.) for which people do not need to know each other. The festive occasion is enough to create a celebrating community; and

- the gathering of the local church, which is, by its very nature, open to all: the baptized, catechumens, interested parties, young and old, regulars or visitors, etc. I am speaking of this third kind of gathering, which best signifies the church open to and for all, and imbued with a familial spirit.

We must not let ourselves be paralyzed by old outlooks that favored religious entertainment and the voice of choirs but not the assembly's song.

WORDS THAT ARE CHANTED, SUNG AS A PSALM OR SUNG

If the most important revolution of Vatican II was to open the scriptures to the people and proclaim the good news in their own language, the Council also intended to reform Christian initiation and its sacraments in the same spirit. But this is far more complex than translating the Bible.

Here we need to undertake a process of inculturation comparable to that which took place in the fourth century, by Chrysostom in Greek and Augustine in Latin. They initiated their assemblies, the majority of whom were catechumens or the recently baptized, into biblical language and its message. As they did this, they initiated them into the rich symbols of becoming Christian: the rites of the catechumenate, the baptismal washing, the anointing with oil, and the eucharistic meal, and they used the converts' own cultures to do so.

How is this related to liturgical song? The Word is not simply read and explained to the people; rather, the liturgy must afford people every opportunity to hear this word of God. This goes well beyond the content of the words. For example, chanting the word gives it the same kind of background we would hear in a poem that is read poetically. When the psalmist and the whole assembly sing the psalm, they embrace the path laid out by the verses of the psalm. When we sing passages from the scriptures in an antiphon, a refrain or a troparion, the melody enlarges the meaning of the words.

Almost all of these practices have disappeared from ordinary French culture, with the exception in certain instances of children's nursery rhymes. Thanks to the liturgy, different styles of festive, poetic and sacred speech are coming to life again. Both meanings of inculturation are at work here.

THE PEOPLE'S AUTHENTIC SONG

There were two pillars to the liturgical renewal in the Catholic Church in the twentieth century: rediscovering the Bible and participating through song in the liturgical action.

The people's religious song existed in the songs used in devotions, but they were the exception in sung Masses. From the time of the reforms on, the people found their voice again in the liturgy itself.[60]

---

[60] When in the 1950s we began singing the psalms in French in the Sunday liturgy, a cultured person said to me, "This is the totally wrong way to go. Today, people don't sing; they listen to people who know how to sing." One might say that today's widespread use of song in Sunday gatherings in France represents a real cultural revolution.

In order for this to have happened, we had to create a great number of songs, texts, and music that were appropriate for the rites of the Mass. It was essential that the assembly be able to sing them. Here again the ongoing cultural revolution is important and significant. As we have seen, for long centuries singing in Latin at Mass was the domain of musicians. Because of this, returning their song to the people has not been an easy battle. To the ears of many church musicians, what we were producing was not music.

True enough, once French was used in the liturgy, we went from one extreme to the other. Between 1968 and 1970, people took as their frame of reference for popular liturgical music the contemporary music of the media, complete with percussion and syncopation. But this was only the veneer of inculturation; it borrowed a certain style without any profound exchange between the gospel and the religious soul of the people. Contemporary twelve-tone or post-twelve-tone compositions have remained at the fringes of liturgical renewal because they are too elitist.

Thus, if we are going to undertake the work of real inculturation, our only option is to begin with the rite itself, as we have tried to do throughout this book, in conjunction with genuine dialogue with the assemblies concerned about human and religious significance of the rites.

PATHS THAT ARE TOO SHORT

Because inculturation takes place at deep levels, such work is slow; it has many pitfalls, and takes place far away from the public eye. We have already indicated several dead-ends. Let us look at two other problematic solutions.

The first dead-end is using publication or distribution by the media as the only standard for choosing music. It is deemed successful because it's easy and people like it. People quickly tire of and quickly forget most of this repertoire. There was no guarantee of in-depth exchange between this music and the response of faith and prayer by these assemblies. We may have even discouraged them in the short term.

A second avenue is more positive, but may be inadequate. It consists in distributing only those pieces that experts have selected for their musical and literary value. While all songs chosen should be liturgically and musically credible, their value also depends on how the assembly receives them. The repertoire of centuries that has been passed down to us is the result of both tacit consensus and recognized acceptance. Just think of the four sequences retained from among the thousands created during the Middle Ages.

Those responsible for liturgical ministry, and most especially for the song of the assembly, should work closely with the assembly to be able to feel with the assembly what invites it into the mystery and what does not. I call this — please forgive the jargon — the assembly's self-inculturation.

THE BENEFITS OF SELF-INCULTURATION

Rather than give a theoretical definition of self-inculturation, let me give you a concrete example to help you understand what I mean.

I was named pastor of five parishes where I had to celebrate with very small assemblies made up of people of all ages and different levels of culture. They used a repertoire of songs that had no lasting value, but which people sang willingly at liturgy. I did not want to impose a new repertoire of my own choosing, so I tested a few songs that met the necessary textual and musical criteria. I wanted to see which ones would be accepted, learned easily, sung by heart, would not wear out, and would create a real ambiance of communal prayer for the different times and parts of the celebration.

Some pieces were well-received, but after some time, voices fell off and people were just going through the motions. On the other hand, some pieces that had demanded a lot of commitment and which initially met with no enthusiasm eventually took hold and were sung easily and with relish. After 18 years, I had a feel from the assembly as to which songs were tired and which should be kept. This is what I call self-inculturation. These communities tested for themselves what gave life to their celebrations and nourished their faith.

This has enabled me to observe, among other things, the permanent value of certain traditional forms of popular French melodies (old noëls, Breton airs, etc.), and the value of what has been created using these same rhythmic and melodic models.[61] Real inculturation of this kind exists insomuch as it is true that art is always re-creation, never absolute creation.

The fruit of the slow work of osmosis among local congregations that celebrate the best will be a body of the best-received, the longest-lasting, and the most liturgical songs.

FROM THE CORPORAL TO THE MUSICAL

Physical behaviors and all their attendant symbolism represent the deepest aspect of a culture, and the one that is the most difficult to unlock. For example,

---

[61] When you give these "re-creations" to children, young people and ordinary adults, they get into them without ever suspecting that these pieces have secular roots. This means that today we have a job of inculturation to do that has never been done for the liturgy in French, with the exception of the Genevan Psalter from the Reformed tradition.

people can be totally lost in the liturgy of the Byzantine church, even though its fundamental development is the same as that of our Roman Mass. The language of gestures is more resistant to cultural change than spoken language.

How does this aspect of liturgical celebration touch on songs and music? In so far as our congregations are engaged in profound changes in ritual behaviors, it touches on the styles of song and their length. Before Vatican II, the Roman liturgy was fully ritualized. The rubrics[62] gave precise instructions about how each rite was to be carried out, how each gesture was to be made, where the priest was to stand, and which direction he should face. In contrast, the songs that were sung during these rites were only loosely attached to them. The rubrics were silent about the ritual behaviors of the faithful. It seemed that everyone assisted at Mass in the way that seemed best to them, even though they were conditioned by what their social milieu judged acceptable.

A profound change was ushered in when the members of the assembly themselves were designated as actors in the rites, and ministers were given more leeway as to their stance, their gestures, their tone of voice, and so on. Nonetheless, the rites in general, even since the reform, have not lost their rigidity. Despite the removal of certain things, people often feel overwhelmed by words to say, things to do and songs to sing. Hence the reflection, "We no longer have time to pray."

TAKE TIME TO PRAY BETTER IN SONG

In contrast to older people, some young people and some new Christians are asking for long periods of silence, meditation, contemplation and song. "How can we sing so many different songs at Mass?" (There are about ten, not including the dialogues and acclamations). "We would prefer longer songs that create a real time for prayer rather than a bunch of little bits that are gone before we've even gotten into them."

This is a serious question, all the more so because we live in such a fast-paced society. Images, sounds and news all flash by, leaving only fleeting impressions. A close-knit monastic community that is already well acquainted with the songs can string together many pieces that act as a kind of well-tilled soil in which the seed that sprang from the word of God can flourish. But the ordinary folk of the local parish whose understanding of Christian symbols is very limited need time to get into the ritual movement, and through it come to adoration, petition, praise and the silence in which the Spirit speaks to the human heart.

It is there that the slow and always unfinished work of inculturating Christian rites unfolds.

---

[62] Rules governing the way in which the rites should be performed. They are printed in red in the liturgical books, in contrast to texts to be spoken, which are printed in black.

Postlude

WHAT EAR HAS NOT HEARD

It has happened that at a given liturgy the songs were correctly performed, the readings read intelligently, and the rites performed carefully. Still the whole thing was cold and boring. What was missing?

What was missing was the essential: a dynamism that comes from the breath of the Spirit, the aching of desire for a message that sets us free, the joy of knowing in hope that we are saved, a fervor in our petitions to the God of all goodness, the warmth of a family gathered together, an assembly that is alive with its expectation of the coming of the reign of God, a genuine alleluia of thanksgiving....

It is the nature of liturgy that the invisible is only revealed in the visible; what lies beyond comes to us only in the here and now of symbols, postures, words... and sounds! What is necessary is a meeting between the desire that wells up in us and the grace that is offered from above.

What is true of a musical performance is also true of a liturgical song; the listeners, forgetting both the sounds and the interpreter, are carried away to the point where they sometimes say, "It was sublime." An essential difference remains, however: in the liturgy, even if the church is poor, the preacher simple, and the voices of the singers not quite together or on key, a miracle can always happen. What the eye cannot see, what the ear cannot hear, what our hands cannot do, happens here and now because of the faith of sisters and brothers gathered together and the breath of the Spirit that brings to life the new creation in the risen Christ.

Similarly, a homilist tells himself, "I am neither an orator nor an intellectual, but the Spirit is with me to announce the good news." The presider says, "My gestures can hardly suffice to make present here what the Lord did at the Last Supper, but he does this through me for those who will share in this bread." The cantor says, "My voice isn't very beautiful, but if the Spirit plays me like a harp between his fingers, I will sing the right notes and my prayer will take wings."

Each member of the assembly thinks, "Our assembly finds it really hard to sing to God a worthy song of praise. But in communion with all those who have been saved, our song will rise as with one voice to our most high God."

> *From our inner life wells up a hymn.*
>
> *The spirit that is alert hears the word.*
>
> *From unquenchable desire bursts forth ardent prayer.*

By and in the liturgy each rite, each word, each sound is called to become the church's inspired song that gives all glory to God while it makes humanity holy.

> *To sing the praise of the God who is beyond all words,*
>
> *to sing a psalm in response to God's inspired word,*
>
> *to give voice to human pain,*
>
> *to burst forth in the thanksgiving of those who have been raised to new life*
>
> *infinitely surpasses even the most poignant and refined*
>
> *musical artistry of human beings.*
>
> *For in the voice of the church at prayer*
>
> *we hear the song of the beloved to his Father;*
>
> *on the breath of the Spirit of love*
>
> *rises up, in every language and dialect,*
>
> *the groaning of our death-bound universe*
>
> *for the new creation,*
>
> *in union with the heavenly hymn of all the saved*
>
> *who without end sing the song of Moses,*
>
> *a song old and ever new:*
>
> *"Let us sing to the Lord,*
>
> *he has covered himself in glory!"*